SCARS

THE ROADMAP TO THE SOUL

A Pastoral Reflection

Maxine Lloyd, MDiv MSPC, LGPC

ML Ministries
Email: mlministries@isaacministriesinc.org

Cover Design by KK Productions
Editor: E. Claudette Freeman

Library of Congress Control Number: 2019905522

Published by ML Ministries
P.O. Box 2621
Ellicott City, MD 21041
(240) 476-7700

Printed in the United States of America
ISBN-13: 978-0-9800226-1-2
ISBN-10: 0-980226-1-4

A TRIBUTE TO

DEACON JOHN H. LLOYD, SR.
My Daddy and My Hero

Acknowledgements

This book is dedicated to my loving and wonderful earthly father who demonstrated the love and character of my Heavenly Father. I thank you daddy for loving me unconditionally when I know I was not always obedient or respectful to you in my formative years. But, your love, patience, selfless giving, and sacrifices embodied Jesus, the Son of God; who gave His life as the sacrificial lamb for the sins of the world. I love and miss you so much. Nevertheless, I know I am in good hands. God, my Heavenly Father, shows me more and more your journey to unconditional love. The seed He planted long ago in your heart, came to full maturity. Your mission here with us was complete and God called you home. My journey continues until I fulfill my mission here on earth.

Thank you to my mother, who I thought left this world much too soon, for the love and care she provided to her nine children, grandchildren, and great-grandchildren. You have left a legacy that we all pattern and mimic in the kitchen in some way or another. Your grandchildren constantly remind me that their grandmother wasn't like I am when it comes to keeping their kids. But I think I have moved towards being more like you when it comes to that.

I am grateful to my siblings and the sibling rivalry we have shared, for you have helped to shape my character, personality, resilience, and strength in more ways than you can imagine. To all my relatives, friends now, and those that I will meet soon; we are all interconnected and bound together through a common shared bond, the love of God.

Thanks to my new-found friend and editor, E. Claudette Freeman, who stretched me and encouraged me to write. To write even when I didn't have words. The moral of her story she shared with me was "royal word" which reminded me that I had a story that many are waiting to hear. They are royal words because they are from the King of Kings and Lord of Lords. I pray what I have become, the Master will say, "well done!" Thank you, Dr. Vikki Johnson, for introducing me to such a wonderful and inspiring editor.

Last, but not least, thank you to my children and grandchildren. We have been through some tough times, estranged at times, but God. I know that God is not through with us yet, and this last year has drawn us closer together than ever before. I love you all so much and know that God is able to do exceedingly abundantly above all we can ask or think; according to the power that worketh in us. With God, all things are possible; if we only believe.

Maxine Lloyd

Abstract

Discovering your life purpose is often an elusive and uncertain journey. I believe there are people who live most of their life and never discover their purpose. I continuously ask myself what the meaning behind the adversity is I often face; and why do bad things have to happen to me. The more I looked for meaning and answers it seemed the more trouble I found. In spite of the trouble, I was always resilient and bounced back. I would take the lemon and make lemonade and stones cast at me became steppingstones that escalated me high above my enemies. It seemed most of my trials I had to face alone because family and friends were not around. This was all part of God's plan for my life. My purpose was to experience sorrow, suffering, and pain so that I could know without a shadow of a doubt that God alone would deliver me. Yes, He used many people to assist me; but, ultimately His love, grace, and good will towards me were the only things I found would outlast anything or anyone else. It was through these trials that I found my purpose and meaning of life in service to God and the world. The foundation of desiring to help others was discovered through my own profound and personal life experiences. Thus, my personal life experiences are eyewitness accounts of how my biopsychosocial, spiritual, and political formation steeped in trauma propelled me into a career of helping relationships. My story of scars is how an epigenetic view of how traumatic experiences can shape a love story that leads to the discovery of life purpose and meaning. Understanding and embracing life's most challenging experiences make the difference between resilience and despair. Jesus' life, as narrated in the bible, is the epitome of a life lived in shame and suffering. Yet, He gave His life as a ransom so that others could live life and live it more abundantly. This is my life purpose and destiny. If I can help somebody along the way, then I will know my living was not in vain.

SCARS

THE ROADMAP TO THE SOUL

A Pastoral Reflection

Maxine Lloyd, MDiv MSPC, LGPC

Foreword

In Maxine Lloyd's *Scars: The Roadmap to the Soul*, Rev. Lloyd reveals how you can rise above the cinders of your charred, broken childhood, and abusive relationships; and allow God to create a new creation. Maxine is an example of what can happen when you place yourself and your pain on The Potter's wheel and allow Him to transform you into something wonderful; "meet for The Masters use".

Rev. Lloyd reveals how she allowed her scars to be the connection to others in their healing process. Her trials and triumphs have taken her on a road to self-awareness, and her insight allows her to clearly discern issues in the clients she serves. In her role as a Pastoral Counselor, she walks you into the lives of three of her clients and reveals how she uses her life experiences to intervene in the woundedness of those guided to her to begin the process of scaring. Scars are where we've been, but how we decide to use them determines where we are going.

Scars: The Roadmap to the Soul is both inspiring and informative and generates hope for healing.

Gail Bethea-Jackson; LCW-C

Table of Contents

Introduction – Metaphor of Pastoral Counseling

"There is no fear in love; but perfect love casts out fear, because fear involves torment. But he who fears has not been made perfect in love."
(1 John 4:18)

Hannah Hurnard's *Hinds Feet on High Places* is an allegory with a spiritual meaning relayed through figurative language about pain, love, and suffering. It is a symbolic narrative about the struggles, trials, evils, and disappointments we all go through. The characters, Much-Afraid, Mrs. Dismal Foreboding, Gloomy, Spiteful, and Craven Fear are members of the Fearing Family who live in the Village of Much Trembling. There are other characters, Chief Shepherd, Mercy, Peace, and Much-Afraid's fellow workers, who work in the Shepherd's field, Valley of Humiliation. The Fearing Family characters represent our narrative to life events as we live from day to day with many struggles.

However, Much-Afraid, who has been in the service of the Chief Shepherd is invited to leave the Valley of Humiliation, where the Chief Shepherd had great flocks pastured, and follow Him to the High Places. Much-Afraid decides to escape from her Fearing family and friends to follow Chief Shepherd to the High Places where perfect love casts out fear. Much-Afraid's journey leads her through tumultuous paths, hardships unspeakable, and times of loneliness, when she felt the Chief Shepherd had left her alone in her fear and pain.

Transformation only comes when she believes in the Chief Shepherd (as we must do), perseveres, endures the hardships, and accepts that with love comes pain. If we would know love, we must know pain.

"Then will you let me plant the seed of true Love [in your heart] now?" asked the Shepherd. "It will take you some time to develop hinds' feet and to climb to the High Places, and if I put the seed in your heart now it will be ready to bloom by the time you get there." Much-Afraid shrank back. "I am afraid," she said. "I have been told that if you really love someone you give that loved one the power to hurt and pain you in a way nothing else can." "That is true," agreed the Shepherd. "To love does mean to put yourself into the power of the loved one and to become very vulnerable to pain, and you are much-afraid of pain, are you not?" She nodded miserably and then said shamefacedly, "Yes, very much afraid of it." "But it is so happy to love," said the Shepherd quietly.

"It is happy to love even if you are not loved in return. There is pain, too, certainly, but Love does not think that very significant" (Hurnard, 2012, p. 9).

"Scars are the roadmap to the soul" (e-reading work-sheets.com) and the soul is where love abides. This metaphor alerts me to the fact that true love is shaped through the road of adversity. The word love is often used to mean a feeling or an emotion. Like feelings that come and go; people are said to fall in and out of love. Conversely, the true demonstration of love is an action. *"For God so loved the world that He gave His only begotten Son, that whoever believes in Him should not perish but have everlasting life"* (John 3:16). The scars that Jesus received on His body were the roadmap to His soul. The soul is where our passion lies. It is the seat of our consciousness, our thoughts and our motivations. Where our passion is, is where we extend acts of love and care. Agape love is the unconditional love that allowed Jesus to pay the ultimate sacrifice for our sins. This love never ends but continues to grow from the seed planted and it never loses its power to save and to heal.

In the Beginning

I carried many painful, stressful, and shameful memories of my past for most of my life. The worst of them was my experience of being in a violent relationship. The relationship not only caused physical, psychological, and emotional pain, but brought the culmination of my life development of pain and abuse full circle. The abuse didn't just start in my 23-year marriage. It started in middle childhood. The experiences from early childhood and into an emerging adult compromised the Christian religious values I was taught, believed and embraced as the foundation of my lifestyle development. Yet, my belief in God sustained me and built in me the ego strength I needed to survive.

At the age of around seven or eight an older family member molested me. I was merely a child learning how to navigate friendships and become socially acceptable within peer groups and family members. The molestation left me feeling ashamed and guilty. I felt I was less than the other girls, inferior, and damaged. We attended church every Sunday and my father held official roles in the church. The bible stories learned in Sunday school laid the foundation of how I would use and build my stages of faith.

My menstrual cycle started late, which made me a late bloomer. Therefore, all the other physical body changes of development came late. The most noticeable signs of puberty for girls, around the ages of nine to 11, are height and weight increase, breast growth, pubic hair appears, and hair appears under the arm. Even hips become shapely. The changes in this growth spurt is extremely noticeable to children when comparing their bodies to their friends. Here I was at the age of 12 still looking like a little girl. I was ashamed of my body and condemning myself for not being able to fit in. I could not talk to my mom about anything. My only saving grace was one of my older sisters, who helped me with getting the right supplies to care for myself during my menstrual cycle. As I look back over my late childhood years, developing friendships was lacking. Even now, my inability to make friends then, continues to have an impact on how I enter and remain engaged in friendships. Since I was not as mature looking or as popular as the other girls, I was not included in their peer group.

This perceived rejection continued throughout middle and high school. I compensated for my peers' rejection by having my own peer group of friends that were not a part of the in-crowd. Our group was smart, intelligent, cute, shapely in our own way, but not flirty or loose. Yet, I was attracted to the roughnecks, guys who were popular, some football players (who were not very smart and treated their girlfriends bad), but nevertheless, cool. I struggled during these years trying to reconcile my religious values and beliefs with my biological, social, emotional, and psychological development processes that were at war within me. I became rebellious like my older siblings. I lied to my parents about where I was going. I was skipping school, smoking, and drinking. All the while, I was never comfortable with doing any of these things. I was laden with guilt, shame, and felt so inferior and oppressed inside my body.

I was constantly filled with anxiety and negative self-talk about my body image, my failed attempts at having a relationship that was enriching and not toxic, and thoughts of not being good enough. I was never good enough and never would be. My friends' homes were nicer, and their parents were cool. There were always arguments, if not between siblings, between my mom and dad. I was looking for love, and as the cliché goes, in all the wrong places. I couldn't wait to get out on my own so that my life would be better. Most of my sex education was through what I got in school, either from peers or sex education classes.

How Did I Get Here?

It was during my adolescence years and throughout my emerging adult years, I began to notice more of how I was treated differently than other children who may have been in school, in stores, and in general public settings. I always had the desire to be better and to fit in. I thought I could accomplish this by being smart in school. I was behaving like the perfect child, trying not to get into trouble with friends, displease my parents, and being respectful in all my relationships with people who I perceived had power over me. My early adulthood years brought more shame and uncertainty of social and interpersonal relationships, as I experienced acquaintance rape and emotional turmoil in my boyfriend/girlfriend relationships. I married my abuser and became the major breadwinner in our household working a middle management position. In corporate America, I learned it wasn't what you knew, but who you knew and the color of your skin that determined your access into networks that took you to higher levels of management, success, and money. It was there I learned about racial discrimination. I worked my way up the corporate ladder, but I noticed and felt the discrimination I received from the "good ole boy network". I still was not good enough.

I paid a dear price for having the lack of knowledge, resources, and understanding of the political powers that were at work building my social construct of oppression. I hated politics and felt I would never get involved in them because of what I thought were the injustices, game playing, and destruction to peoples' lives it caused. I didn't like all the injustices I felt, but could not name, but I knew that I had to do something about it for myself and for others. People would always come to me to talk about their problems and hurts, and for advice about life's hardships. I think they understood my faith and knew the scriptures were the solutions to my issues and helped to sustain me through the most challenging times in my life. I guess they thought if my faith could sustain me through some of the worst crises of life, they could make it through as well.

My identity achievement, which means, I had to go through some very chaotic and traumatic experiences and come to understand and commit to who I was. Doing so meant merging my negative experiences and embarking on a path that ultimately would assist others who have or would pass my way with similar life stories.

The scars from my past have catapulted me into my future of Pastoral Counseling (PC). On my journey through life, I was always afraid and anxious. I experienced deep hurts, but through it all I was taught love, forgiveness, and acceptance of people and circumstances that wounded me in the most profound ways. Demonstrating God's unconditional love is to embody love in my relationships with humanity, by understanding their make-up and how they have become who they are, and how I can help them move from places of despair and hopelessness to faith, hope, and love. Unconditional love shapes my life message.

A life message is a signpost that reveals to others who you really are, and it speaks to your meaning and purpose in life (Willis, 1996, p. 10). My life message is the total experience from which I speak with authority because I have done or experienced what I have spoken. I am the expert on my own life. Rick Johnson (2013) affirms the focus of the pastoral counselor (PC) is to be open to the unique ways that experience is defined and how people access life-affirming beliefs and practices. Boundaries are often crossed between the sacred and the secular. However, the PC purports the unifying idea that embracing a loving and compassionate heart allows people to make decisions based on joy and abundance instead of fear and scarcity. People should live in the freedom to choose whether sacred or secular means bring them to a life affirming existence of health and well-being.

My life goal is to live life in such a way that I am an instrument in God's hand to be used to help others. Thus, my life goals require me to be vigilant about being open to diverse theories, philosophies and religions. How do I understand and process my access and ability to get the resources I need for health and well-being? The scars I carry are the roadmap to how love came to abide in my soul. Soul is defined as the seat of my consciousness, my thoughts, and my motivation. Kenneth Pargament (2007) defines the psyche as the soul. I desire love to be the essence of my thoughts, my heart or passion, and the motivation of why I do the things that I do. My spirituality communicates my values and beliefs. My values and beliefs impact all that I do. And in all I do, I strive to do all to the glory of God. *"Love is patient, love is kind, it does not seek its own, is not provoked, thinks no evil, bears all things, believes all things, hopes all things, endures all things, love never fails"* (1 Corinthians 13). I love God with all my heart, soul, mind and strength; and love my neighbor as myself. Love does no harm to his neighbor. This is captured in the PC's ethical principle of "do no harm".

My call to be a pastoral counselor is to bring restoration of health, well-being, healing, liberation and hope to a population of people whose unalienable rights have been compromised by their strategies for survival. In the United States, the Declaration of Independence propagates, "We hold

11

these truths to be self-evident, that all men are created equal, that they are endowed by their Creator with certain unalienable rights that among these are life, liberty and the pursuit of happiness." What does unalienable mean? In Black's Law Dictionary, unalienable "means incapable of being alienated, that is, sold or transferred." You cannot surrender, sell or transfer unalienable rights because they are a gift from the Creator to the individual and cannot under any circumstances be surrendered or taken. All individuals have unalienable rights. Nevertheless, there are inalienable rights; rights which are not capable of being surrendered or transferred without the consent of the one possessing such rights as found in, Morrison v. State, Mo. App., 252 S.W. 2d 97, 101 (Unalienable Rights). Many people have consented or been compromised to surrender or transfer their unalienable rights to live in the potential that God created them in order to survive. Victims of domestic violence and child abuse who have been repeatedly threatened with death or the hurt of a loved one, surrender their rights in exchange for life and safety of themselves or others.

Where Is This Road Leading Me?

Today we live in a world that is filled with hate, suffering, sorrow, disease, and poverty. Our relationships have been challenged, and in some cases, shattered to the point where some feel there is no hope for healing. We are afraid of one another, we are afraid of how we will survive from day-to-day, and we are afraid of global war and terrorism which have become the norm on daily news programs. The tragedies faced throughout the world are at astronomical proportion as we hear of global natural disasters, social upheavals, psychological trauma, family and world moral decline, and increased divorces.

Pastoral counseling provides the framework to help navigate and decipher the roadmap that will lead us to a safe place that promotes health and well-being. A roadmap guides you to a destination and keeps you on track so that you do not get lost or confused as to where you are at any given time. A roadmap will also give you landmarks, and important resource stops that may be needed on your journey, so you know how to plan, when it is time to refuel, make sure personal needs are met and find detours and alternative routes when we hit dead ends and/or get stuck.

13

Earlier I defined my soul as the seat of my consciousness, my thoughts, and my motivation. The metaphor I chose, scars are the roadmap to the soul; and the soul is where love abides speaks to my formation as a pastoral counselor. The scars are the results of the experiences of trauma and other negative experiences. Each experience was a marker on the roadmap that helped that seed of love to grow despite the adversity. The experiences helped shape my worldview, revealed how I was to connect to my purpose, and how I was to make meaning out of things that had happened. Becoming aware of one's worldview, values, belief system, and cultural context is an important aspect of being a skilled therapist (Wiggins, 2009, p. 59). The experiences also helped to shape my strategies for survival. The experiences will direct me to my destiny; when I reach it love will be perfected in who I was meant to be.

The Microsoft Thesaurus (2010) defines a scar as "a mark from a blemish to disfigurement." It can also be defined as an effect, such as a wound, hurt, trauma, or after-effect. Lastly, a scar can be defined as damage, such as hurt, affect, or a scratch. How we respond to the experiences will determine how we define the scar. Is it a mark that we receive, an effect or result of something, or is it damage done to us? Who I have become is manifested in the way I understand my purpose, the meaning of the experiences I have faced, and choosing to embrace love and allow it to reside inside of me.

Arrived! Here at My Destiny

I have been much afraid most of my life because of not being born and raised in an elaborately-enriched environment. I lived in anxiety and fear due to domestic disputes inside and outside of my home. We were economically challenged, and my health care was lacking in many areas. I was an introvert, and my inner thoughts guided my actions and behavior. However, the one thing that blessed my life, grounded me, and built my resiliency was being introduced to God at an early age. My relationship with God guided me to peaceful moments, helped me resolve spiritual struggles, and built my faith to believe that I could overcome my condition.

Prayer, meditation, music, and learning the scriptures of the bible were the interventions that I started to practice at an early age. However, setting boundaries, risk-taking, self-care, fasting, and education were not part of my arsenal of survival strategies until I became a middle-aged adult. As I began expanding my education, I added more tools in my treasure chest that helped along the way. Education introduced me to a new circle of influence of people and my social skills increased. Nonetheless, I added more scars to my journey. The more scars I added, the more my soul cried out for liberation from the pain, the hurt, the suffering. As mentioned earlier, the scar that left a mark, became an effect, and caused the most damage, was domestic violence. It was this scar that introduced me to counseling.

The roadmap took me to the place of refueling, rest stops, and places to gain nourishment- spiritually and physically. I became more acquainted with my faith, God, and liberation theology in seminary. I was introduced to pastoral counseling while in seminary by a colleague who was a pastoral counselor. It was through the pastoral counseling program that the seed of love started to bear fruit. As I learned how to be a pastoral counselor, I opened myself up to heal from the past trauma and to start my journey on the road to love. Through stories shared by my colleagues, insight and guidance in supervision, knowledge from my professors, help from the staff, my own psychotherapy, and my sessions with my clients, I embraced love, compassion, empathy, listening, hope, purpose, meaning, and all the issues of life in new ways. It wasn't the situations that changed, but the changes took place in me, and changed who I was to become. I was freed from a lot of baggage that I have carried for most of my life. I came to understand how I had developed and how I was crippled in my formative years. I understood how my body worked and the impact of responses that I had no control over, but were hard wired, created to work for a specific purpose. I was educated on how thoughts affect behavior and how patterns of thought evolve unconsciously.

This empowered me to release guilt, anxiety, and fear that manifested in my body as physical symptoms, as well as, challenged me psychologically, emotionally, and spiritually. I let go of anger and offered forgiveness and accepted forgiveness.

These are issues that bring clients to counseling. Taking an intercultural approach to understanding the whole person who is sitting across from me, means I respect who they are and how they have been influenced by their environment and family interactions. The awareness of environmental factors and the various governmental and societal systems' impact can bring holistic therapeutic interventions that are needed in treating the whole person. Unlike that of spiritual directors, whose primary focus is to help guide one's attention to their spiritual life in relationship to God or a higher power, as a pastoral counselor I help resolve conflicts, work to restore mental health, and bring healing to trauma victims. Spiritual direction is defined as the interaction between one person, trained to listen for the movement of God, and another who desires to develop and cultivate an intimate, personal relationship with God (Tisdale, Doehring, & Lorraine-Poirier, 2003, p. 53). Pastoral counselors are learning how to integrate spirituality in therapeutic interventions. Voices from various fields of study, such as quantum physics, systems science, psychology, communications science, and ecology, are joining and supporting the Eastern philosophical view that all of life is

18

interconnected by dynamic patterns of energy (Johnson, 2013). As a Christian, I call this energy the Holy Spirit. Others may say it is intuition or a sixth sense. No therapist can reasonably deny following hunches, experiencing sudden insights, choosing directions without really knowing why or having uncanny feelings that turn out to be of great importance for therapy (Welling, 2005). Nevertheless, the idea is it is a power greater than us that brings about a knowing, an understanding of things that cannot be rationalized, theorized, or explained. PCs see the need to understand these phenomena to be able to grasp the intercultural way of being, understanding, and intervening with their clients.

I am beginning to be intentional about crossing cultural boundaries by thinking, envisioning and entering into the experiences of others' thoughts and feelings even though their feelings and thoughts arise from other frames of reference and moral reasoning (Lartey, 2003). In pastoral counseling possessing the skills to enter into a client's world and how it feels to be them, while appreciating and understanding the nuances and complexities of their lives (from their point of view) is a must. The scars that form their roadmap to the suffering of their souls are better understood when I can see through the lens of unconditional love and unconditional positive regard. Thus, the client's humanity is acknowledged, and the connectedness and interrelatedness give me a broader and expanded understanding of how the experience of trauma, hunger, depression, abuse, substance abuse and other mental health challenges impact their soul. In addition, scars remind us that we have been through meaningful challenges, but we have survived.

From this vantage point, the seed of love continues to grow in me. The work that is being done in my clients is also working a magnificent work within me. I am influenced and made better. The pain I may have experienced, the scars that I continue to carry take on new meaning and new perspective as the fear lessens and I discover my own healing wrapped up in and tied to my clients' healing. I am transformed as my heart is more open to respect our differences and embrace our similarities that create the bond of spiritual oneness, I am you and you are me (Lartey, 2003). Nevertheless, I must create healthy boundaries that promote self-care and not lose the person God created me to be. I am aware of my limitations and the risks of becoming enmeshed in the darkness that can engulf me if I am not practicing my own mindfulness, finding my own sacred space, and resolving my own conflicts and concerns.

Chapter I – Spirituality of Pastoral Counseling

Reflection of the Sacred – Faith Development

God is sacred. Time or space cannot contain God's vastness. God is eternal and has always existed. The Bible, in John 4:24 reads, "*God is a spirit, and those who worship Him, must worship in spirit and truth.*" I believe - by faith - that I was created in the image of God, given a body, soul, and God's Spirit. Thus, the sacredness of the Triune God (God the Father, God the Son, and God the Holy Spirit), express the sacredness of my life and living. This holy union promotes a spiritual connectedness of unconditional love with the sacred that is so powerful and transcendent that words cannot explain it.

Nevertheless, I reflect on the numerous ways that God has revealed His sacredness and the sanctity of my own life in relationship with the created world and heaven. When my body dies and returns to the ground, heaven is the prepared place where my soul will spend eternity with God. The essence of who I am is proven by the tangible things that I can accomplish through God's infinite presence, mighty power, and prayer. God as Spirit allows me to know Him in His

22

characteristics of healer, comforter, father, protector, disciplinarian, and provider from day-to-day. God is not only known, but God is also omniscient, all knowing of all things. God knows me, understands me, and loves me despite me. Although I experience challenges, I realize how resilient and strong I am as I struggle to make sense out of the evil and trials, I face through the revealed word that has guided me throughout my life. And, I have come to respect and to love all things that God created as good, but has in many ways brought hatred, disrespect, and loathing to God's name; particularly, people of all races, religions, and political powers. The diversity of values and beliefs about holy wars, abuse, and the atrocities that families face in trying to survive, are often met with, "how can a loving God allow such terrible things happen to good people?"

The love of God is what makes God astounding and awesome to me. God made everything for humanity to enjoy and cherish as His creation. When I see world hunger, chaos in wars, murder, and torrential storms that destroy lives and property I am saddened by these things. However, my hope is renewed when I see new life springing forth in the birth of a newborn baby, or a rainbow appears in the sky, the sun rises and the sun sets bringing forth a new day, and I remember the promises of His word, the end is not yet.

The revelation that God has a relationship with all creation is also shown in the beauty of snow-covered trees; the rustling waves of the ocean that knows how far to come upon the shore; the awe-inspiring music of Handel's Messiah; the great artistic works of Picasso and Michelangelo, and the gentle breeze of the wind.

I do not know where the wind comes from, but its calming effect enables me to lift my hands in worship to Jehovah Elohim, the Sacred Creator of all things and in whom all things exist. My relationship with the Sacred gives purpose and meaning to my life in a spiritual bond that cannot be broken, not even in death.

Spirituality of Pastoral Counseling

Spirituality is a motivational drive to create a broad sense of personal meaning within an eschatological context. It represents that one's spirituality is the capacity to understand one's life within a broader sense that goes beyond a person's immediate sense of time and place. (Piedmont, 2014).

As spiritual beings, I believe we all share a common bond and heritage that supersedes how we each respond to life. The lens through which I see and experience various aspects of creation; like music, the rustling of leaves, wind that whistles, a sudden feeling of joy, for no reason other than just because is enlightening. I stand in awe watching a sunrise or sunset or seeing a smile. These things tell me all things are interrelated dimensions of who we are. It all breeds a broad respect for others and a corresponding need to protect life in all its forms. My spiritual heritage is derived from being made in the image of my Creator and being steward over all that has been created and entrusted to my care. The beauty of this transcendental power is greater than me and even in the absence of these dimensions; I am conformed to a mysterious power that cannot always be explained. It is this mysterious power that makes for peace and serenity.

Spirituality is a personal sense of meaning in my life, the why and purpose I was created. It is my relationship with God, the sacred, that transcends all understanding of the human psyche. The Assessment of Spirituality and Religious Sentiments (ASPIRES) scale is a very practical assessment tool that is not cost prohibitive and can be done with individuals and groups. Its application can be used across a wide variety of fields, including conducting pastoral and religious assessments, medical outcome research, correlations between religious and spirituality constructs and other psychosocial outcomes. This scale was derived from and guided by experimental, nondenominational, and multi-culturally valid measures for assessing the psychological aspects of spirituality and religiosity for use in clinical, research, and academic contexts (Piedmont & Toscano, 2016). ASPIRES is beneficial for clinical settings, helping clinicians understand clients and their sense of their life purpose and meaning, both in living and end-of-life issues. Particularly, it oriented me to my inner life, the universality, mutuality, and interrelatedness of all things. I live life in accord with values and beliefs that have been shaped by accepting the universality of all things God created. Life is seen as "both and" rather than "either or". Holding the tension of ambiguities in life and doing the necessary work in me, I find personal meaning and satisfaction in a variety of relationships with others who are different than me.

Through prayer, I experience a personal sense of emotional satisfaction, strength, and support in my encounters with God. Intentional time spent in solitude with God fortifies me against dark places that invade my sacred space and desire to engulf me during times of spiritual struggles. Emotional renewal, especially during times of crises and stress, is found in reading and studying scriptures. Through meditation, fasting, and silence I have built higher levels of positive affect, become more psychologically mature, and feel more socially supported by friends and family. Building this inner strength promotes health and well-being along with ego strength and resiliency. When I am in a state of contentment, I am more pleasant, reserved, and sincere.

Crises bring to me doubt, fear, and struggle while trying to maintain my connectedness with God. My perceived separation leads to anxiety, dissatisfaction, irritability, and cognitive distortions of God's love and care, and my failures of doing the right thing. Disturbing questions and emotions cause me to doubt my place and purpose in the world and with God. I am resistant to face the inevitable and limited power I have over my life (Pargament, 2007). Spirituality can be a resource or a roadblock. The metaphor "coping" has been used to describe the psychological stereotype that religion is inevitably passive, defensive, and maladaptive. Conversely, Pargament (2007) suggests religion as a positive resource to people in times of stress; and the interplay of the person facing critical problems in the context of a larger social milieu. This resonates with me as I grapple with life problems that often invade my peace and I have seen manifest in the life of people. As the wise King Solomon writes, there is nothing new under the sun. The Bible is full of stories of men and women who have faced life struggles, psychologically and theologically, and have found healing and victory.

Understanding the psychological and theological aspects of who we are and what we experience in life stem from the Garden of Eden. Man's - and woman's - relationship with God were broken because of their disobedience. A death sentence was pronounced to the world. Yes, the world. Sometimes we miss the fact that death came, not only to humanity, but to the animals, trees and plants. Heaven and earth will pass away. Adam and Eve's disobedience (sin) in the Garden of Eden, caused sin to be passed to all humanity. No wonder Paul, the Apostle, said, *"For we know that the whole creation groans and labors with birth pangs together until now!"* (Romans 8:22)

The consequences of sin caused physical, psychological, social, and spiritual consequences between God and man, man and Satan, man and woman, and man and him/herself. (I use the term man as a neutral gender describing both male and female.) Physical diseases, mental illness, battle between the sexes, and spiritual warfare are the consequences of humanity's disobedience. The shift of choice from desiring God to desiring any other thing than God will cause a break in you and who God designed you to be.

Let's look at King David of Israel, who is known to be the *"apple of God's eye."* The beloved David was anointed and chosen to be King of Israel when he was just a young boy.

The same David that killed the giant, Goliath, with a slingshot and 5 smooth stones. David was bold in his faith and believed in God, and he was prosperous and blessed. While David loved God, trusted God, and was anointed; he, like all humanity, still could not escape from sin.

David experienced depression, guilt, grief, and loneliness. He experienced fear on many occasions. In many of the Psalms, David writes of his anguish, loneliness, fear of his enemies, his heart-cry over sin, and the guilt and grief he struggled with because of it. We know of his huge grief in the loss of two sons, the baby born to Bathsheba, and his son Absalom (2 Samuel 12:15-23, 12:18-33).

David's children turned against him. The trusted King Saul, who David played the harp and sang Psalms to him when King Saul was troubled by evil spirits (1 Samuel 16:14), tried to kill him. David's daughter, Tamar, was raped by her own brother, Amnon (2 Samuel 13:4-20). David was very angry about it, but David did nothing to redeem Tamar's honor. David's other son, Absalom, has Amnon, his brother killed because of the rape of his sister, Tamar. Tamar, who we know through scripture, was shamed, depressed, grieved, and experienced loss of self-worth. Tamar, violated, deceived, and then hated, remained desolate in her brother Absalom's house. And we do not hear of Tamar again. We read of depression, fratricide, grief, adultery, rape, death, low self-esteem and self-worth, fear, anger, and domestic violence, all the issues that bring people to counseling. Things that leave scars, that fester, and cause spiritual and psychological impairments and dysfunction, if not treated and dealt with.

A pastoral counselor is viewed as someone who is the voice of God who can tell her/him what they need to do. But often the truth and answers lie within themselves. In many cases, King David's faith was working as a resource for him. King David had a very strong relationship and faith in God. He was very enthusiastic about his faith in God. Sometimes, even though he prayed a lot, he felt God did not answer him. Many of us also question God, "God, why didn't you stop the bad things that happened to me? Why do bad things happen to good people?"

James W. Fowler (1981) explains the formal characterization of infancy and undifferentiated faith. Fowler purports there being a pre-stage of faith development called undifferentiated faith, where the seeds of trust, courage, hope, and love are fused in an undifferentiated way and contend with sensed threats of abandonment, inconsistencies and deprivation in an infant's environment. This formulation of mutual faith is contingent upon the primary care givers. Failure to supply mutuality of these qualities of faith can result in the infant being locked in a pattern of isolation and threatens all that comes later in faith development. Many clients that come to counseling have not developed trust in their caregivers or the environments they provided. This prevents them from developing trust in themselves, trust in the larger world of meaning surrounding them, and their parents from being able to mediate and parent them toward images of worthy womanhood or manhood (Fowler, 1981 p. 121).

My pastoral approach with clients today would be to help them reframe and understand scriptural references in their proper context. Help them to explore what is their life purpose, what is needed for them to move forward, and to use the strength of their faith to understand self-love. It is strongly suggested the client develop and regain a sense of community within their faith tradition for connectedness and a support system. Navigating and building a faith-community support system; one can begin to reach out and trust some of the people in their environment and allow them to care about themselves while seeking therapy. We see that Tamar isolated herself and lived in despair in her brother's house. King David, Tamar's caregiver, failed to bring restitution and honor to who God created her to become. Instead, a soul tear happened that destroyed her self-worth, her dignity, and will to live in community. Instead, she withdrew from the "beloved community of family and friends" and chose to live in isolation. She could not face the humiliation, shame, and the defilement to her body, soul, and spirit her brother caused in her life.

The sacredness of all human interactions suggests, when one element hurts, we all are impacted by that hurt. Rev. Dr. Martin Luther King, Jr. said, "*All life is interrelated. We are caught in an inescapable network of mutuality; tied in a single garment of destiny. Whatever affects one directly, affects all indirectly. . . I can never be what I ought to be until you are what you ought to be. And you can never be what you ought to be until I am what I ought to be."*

As I sat with clients revisiting the suffering and sorrow of their past life, their scars are as evident as my own. As countertransference rushes over me, I am caught in the web of the client's hurt that affected my own hurt. I realize, I am she. I am he. We are they. We are all intertwined in the stories of the bible. We become the main characters as our experiences in life are portrayed on the pages of the written word.

Who I am and who I ought to be can only be personified in the unconditional love of God. How I exist, how I think, and what I do is informed by how I view the scars I carry because of self-inflicted, as well as other-inflicted wounds. Do I love myself and do I love others sacrificially, in spite of the pain I have suffered? Spirituality integrated into pastoral counseling goes beyond superficial cultural norms of gender, race, religion, sexual orientation, and at times my own myopic point of view as to how culture perpetrates the deeper dimensions of my problems. Spirituality informs my understanding

34

that human hurts, suffering, and oppression can be from bio-psychosocial, political and spiritual causes. My own hurt and suffering have been linked with social, political, economic, biological, psychological, religious/spiritual, and educational systems that we are forced to live within. The feminist thought, the personal is political and the political is also personal, have helped influence my way of intervening to be able to effectively counsel, guide, and empower individuals (Lartey, 2003). By using an ecological systems model, the set of relationships existing between the client and complex systems, surroundings, and environment, intervention can address many of the factors that impact a client's functioning or impairment. An ecological systems model is important to addressing all areas (e.g., social, education, medical, etc.) that may have an effect on a client's behavior, thinking, emotional state, and social relationships.

The universality of the spiritual markers of faith, hope and love, that have been planted as seeds in me grow stronger with each struggle. Through toil and struggle I make progress and the paradox of time also brings patience, forgiveness, growth, and the increased capacity to love in spite of. Sharing my life stories bring new and healthy perspective and reframing of my worldview that has been shaped by trauma and adversity; so as with those who come to counseling as a client. Moving beyond my own culturally encapsulated worldview to a broader expanded understanding of human experience helps me to embrace the global interrelatedness and mutuality of life in its fullest form (Lartey, 2003).

Through my educational study and life experiences I have come to understand quite clearly that truth cannot be understood from books alone or by any written words, but through personal growth and development in understanding, and that things written even in the Bible (Book of Books) can be astonishingly misunderstood while one still lives on the low levels of spiritual experience and on the wrong side of the grave in the high places (Cooper, 2013, p. 212).

African American Culture and Worldview Formation

My explicit focus on spirituality in populations of African American (AA), pre- and post-diaspora Africa, and other countries of African descent is because of its relevancy to my formation as a pastoral counselor and my own experience of being a client in psychotherapy, and how it has helped me recover and heal. While I carry the scars of being wounded, I am reminded to be sensitive to the hurts of others, empathic in my responses, to respect and appreciate each individual for what they bring to my life, and love for the oppressed, marginalized, and poor. I have experienced first-hand the unconditional love that was planted in a heart that cared about my hurt, understood my pain, and desired to relieve my suffering.

One of the critical challenges for people of color is to keep an appreciative attachment to their cultural heritage at the same time engaging that heritage critically to discern both its strengths and vulnerabilities. It is often difficult to sustain an awareness of the richness of ethnic heritage in the context of developing clinical skills in an environment where cultural norms do not affirm and value the differing realities of people of color (Graham, 2006, p. 91).

Experiences of racism and injustice shape the black perspective on how African American Christians struggle with their environment (Graham, 2006, p. 96). It is believed that education and training programs must address the unique cultural heritage of clinicians. Formation processes should challenge internalized patterns of relational development, the ethnocentrism of psychological theory, and the impact of systems upon African Americans and other racial and ethnic identities. Pastoral counselors should be afforded the opportunities for reflection in shared-cultural, as well as multi-cultural groups. The values and norms of differing others affect educational objectives, business practices and the patterns of family and community life. A pastoral counselor's concerns should go beyond black/white and male/female to black, white, Hispanic, Muslim, Asian, Iraqi, gay, lesbian, inner city urban, metro-urban, etc., and intensify the need to challenge formation standards that are rooted in traditional Western thought and practices. Limiting the standards of training to Western cultural superiority and paternalistic systems are said to be ineffective and immoral; and educational systems that assume the cultural superiority of one group over another, along with paternalistically-toned individualism, contribute to the persistence of racism. From this perspective, formation ought to move pastoral counselors beyond a culturally encapsulated worldview to a broader expanded understanding of the human experience. We should understand that we all are created and made from the same Creator as one people. And, due to the diasporas that have been numerous since the beginning of time, environment and established patterns of behavior (culture) have only shaped our physical, social, psychological, and spiritual make-up, but not the foundational make-up of all humanity. There is no such thing as race, but a term purposefully devised and used to separate, divide and put, specifically, African American people in subjection (Kolbert, 2018). African Americans have been denied the birthright as one of all people who are included in the diverse, beautifully, and wonderfully made creation of God.

For most African Americans, issues of justice have been integral to their religious experience. Given the history of slavery and the role of the black church as a refuge for nurture, comfort, and healing, formation strategies must deal with the importance of the black church as a carrier of meaning, possibility and hope. Dale Andrews (2002), in discussing pastoral care in black churches, underscores this point. African

American religious life developed pastoral care in a campaign for meaning and value in life. Black churches concentrated significant effort in nurturing the black person, teaching coping skills, self-worth, and social justice. To this day, the Black church intends to empower the individual to value oneself while living in a society that does not. Experiences of racism and injustice shape the black perspective on how African American Christians struggle with their environment. For people of color, the cultural symbols of nurture, care and empowerment must be integrated into the process of becoming pastoral counselors/psychotherapists as a counterbalance to the inequities that inevitably occur in institutional systems.

It is critical to incorporate the following components in educational systems for pastoral counseling.

1. Educational/training programs must develop ways for incorporating the individual's racial/ethnic legacy as a learning partner in the formation of pastoral counselors. Creative strategies that substantively engage the cultural context as a valued contributor to the tasks of formation increase the potential for critical self-assessment to glean the cultural wisdom. This also

minimizes the potential for splitting off the denied aspects of culture in the face of the "white" dominant paradigm.

2. In addition to students, learners in any setting, including academia, church leadership, and business, should be grouped with persons who share their racial/ethnic history for segments of their training while also encountering others who are different in training modules. Intentional programmatic settings for intra- and inter-cultural dialogue are essential in order to counter the tendency to see one's own values as normative. Interpersonal Relations Groups should provide the emotional container for a progressively authentic sharing of contrasting world views and their antecedents.

3. Any type of program which admits persons from varying cultural backgrounds must also have faculty and supervisors who are from varying cultural backgrounds. Professors and supervisors must reflect racial/ethnic inclusivity beyond token participation in educational and training offerings for all students. Tokenism is racism. Even in formation programs that do not have persons from differing ethnic backgrounds, students would benefit from the presence of persons that do not mirror their cultural reality. It is in the variation of voices that a student can hear their own voice

more clearly as well as to experientially realize that their voice is not the only voice (Graham, 2006, pp. 93-96).

The potential for stressors to negatively affect the counseling relationship and undermine the work of counselors always looms. For African American female counselors, the cultural ethos of caring can add weight to professional responsibilities of empathy and compassion. Literature documents the need for self-care planning among counselors in general. However, the intersection between counselor preparation, health, wellness, and spirituality seems to be a critical aspect of self-care for African American women. Debora Knowles and Rhonda Bryant (2011) found preliminary data that African American women counselors seem particularly susceptible to role overload and role stress.

Pack-Brown, Whittington-Clark, and Parker (2002) note that there is a confluence between race, ethnicity, and helping for African American women and teasing out the most powerful influence is still difficult at best. However, for African American women in general, American society has deeply embedded colonizing images that are consistent with images of African American women since their forced removal from Africa in the 1600s (Bryant, et al., 2003). These images can distort expectations of African American women helpers and lead to the assignment of or taking on too many roles or responsibilities (Knowles and Bryant, 2011, pp. 44-45).

Slipping into Darkness

A basic fact of life is that spirituality can be a part of a solution and/or a part of the problem when it comes to the searching for and living out a relationship with the sacred (Pargament, 2007). Presence of the spiritual dimension can also be felt through its absence, in feelings of loss and emptiness, in questions about meaning and purpose, alienation and abandonment, and in injustice and unfairness (Johnson, 2013). I have felt the sense of alienation and abandonment, as I persisted in my cries of injustice and unfairness about domestic violence and its destructive forces of suffering and darkness in the life of a victim. How do you reconcile spiritual integration in everyday life, when everyday abuse is present?

Spiritual integration begins with understanding the effectiveness of the search for the sacred lies not as a specific belief, practice, emotion, or relationship, but in the degree to which the individual's spiritual pathway and destinations work together in synchrony with each other (Pargament, 2007). The truth in this begins with knowing the "real self". There is a part of everyone that exists at the center of one's being which holds immense potential for growth, health, and creativity, and possesses knowledge about what is life offering and life enhancing. Suffering and darkness occur when we lose and/or are out of touch with the real self, which has psychological and spiritual consequences (Johnson, 2013). We can find ourselves lost from our spiritual center for many reasons and end up in therapy (Johnson, 2013).

Mary Magdalene lived in ancient biblical times, born in the city of Magdala, Israel.

Mary was single, as all implications from the bible is that she never married. Mary was a common name for women in her era, so she was identified and distinguished from the other Mary's of her time by her birthplace, Magdala. Mary lived in

44

a Jewish community where the practicing religion was Judaism. However, she became a faithful follower of Jesus during His ministry on earth. In the bible, little is told about Mary and her personal life other than Jesus delivered her from seven devils.

In order to get a better understanding of Mary of Magdala and her life, I will use an ecological model to form a picture of the struggles, pains, and hurts women would be accustomed to experiencing in her culture. To define ecological, we take the root word ecology. Ecology is the study of relationships existing between any complex set of systems and their environments and surroundings. The systems can include political, social, legal, religion, education, medical, and economic. Seven systems, seven devils (demons).

When I speak of demons, I am referring to spiritual warfare. In my book, *I'm Mad as^at Hell* (Ball, 2006), I discuss spiritual warfare as Satan (also known as the devil), using strongholds to undermine the Christian believer's efforts to live a victorious life. It is the conflict between the forces of

God and forces of Satan (demons) with the goal being the believer's victory in Christ. A stronghold is an idea, a thought process, a habit, or an addiction through which Satan has set-up occupancy in your life—a place where he has the advantage.

To better understand the developmental vulnerabilities of growing up in an environment that is based in systemic, or class-based oppression, we can consider the impact to a person's health and well-being, illness/disease, and psychological/spiritual challenges. There are three categories of strongholds that can be broken down into the systemic oppression that can impact a person's functioning. They are ideological, personal, and cosmic strongholds. Once these strongholds have been set-up in a person's life, a person can lose their sense of self, the person God created with purpose and meaning. Demonic spirits roam throughout the earth seeking a body to inhabit and exercise their evil works. These spirits dwell in the atmosphere until they can find a person susceptible or open to their schemes. This is normally done through the mind. How we think will trigger a feeling. The feeling causes us to display a behavior. Below gives a breakdown where ideologies, oppressions, and spiritual attacks can be an influence and eventually, become hurts, habits, hangups, addictions, and dysfunction.

Ideological Strongholds – are built around systems of thought and ideas that are embodied in cultures and that exert pressure on members of that culture. Through this influence, which the bible calls the world, a whole society begins to hold certain values. What Satan does to individuals through the flesh, he does in society through the world. In time, personal strongholds become embodied in cultures as strongholds. Some examples are manifested as pornography, homosexuality, abortion, gambling, and the religious revolution through New Age Thinking.

Personal Strongholds - areas of our lives in which we are most vulnerable to Satan's attacks. These areas are where Satan always seems to get an advantage over you. These attacks are through the flesh, your inner tendency and capacity to sin. Through the flesh you can be influenced in your mind, your will, and your emotions. Your pride can sometimes keep you in bondage. Satan wants you to depend on yourself and your own strength. We can do it ourselves. We don't need help from anybody. We can just pray it away. I am a strong believer in prayer, but God has given us other tools and Spiritual Gifts in the body of Christ to work in conjunction with prayer. Ephesians 4:27 says, *"Neither give place to the devil."* Don't let Satan have an inch, a toehold, or the slightest chance of influencing you. The slightest inch, or toehold will become a stronghold in your life before you know it.

Cosmic Strongholds – the actual attack of Satan and a group of evil spirits that, with the aid of humanity, establishes a counter-culture of sin defying God's righteous order. Its goal is to oppose God's work, steal, kill, and destroy. In the world around us in the atmosphere lurks evil beings under Satan's leadership. During the latter years of the 20th century, Satan's forces have gained many strongholds in the United States that Americans are acknowledging and have begun to be aware of evil spirits, the occult, mediums, channeling, demon possession, and satanic worship (Willis 1996 pg. 20).

12 For our struggle is not against flesh and blood, but against the rulers, against the authorities, against the powers of this dark world and against the spiritual forces of evil in the heavenly realms (Ephesians 6:12, NIV).

Ancient biblical day societies were patriarchal. The male gender was predominately ruler over everything in society. Women were considered property and valued by their ability to have children. As well, children did not have any rights. The poor in society were considered outcasts, oppressed, marginalized, and disenfranchised. If we look at the life of Mary Magdalene, although she was financially able to help support the ministry of Jesus, she was still a woman.

A look at women today, although many gains have been made, women are still fighting for equal rights in pay, being acknowledged in pulpits, and are still expected to be, as some might say, barefoot and pregnant. A woman of childbearing age today maybe overlooked for promotions or find it hard to break the glass ceiling based on their potential to miss work because of pregnancy. There are some who think they are "putting women in their place" and reminding them they are the weaker vessel, castigating them through domestic violence, sexual harassment in the workplace, sexual assault, rape, and denying the equality of being made in the image of God. Think about these strongholds and reflect on how they manifest in your own life, whether you are male or female.

Despite the prohibitions and restrictions of women in this society, there were several women who defied the patriarchal political climate in which they were doomed to die. Mary Magdalene was one of those women. Impaired by the laws of her culture, despairing of life living with seven evil and demonic spirits, Mary went seeking after that which could deliver and heal her emotional and psychological impairments and dysfunction. She found the Wonderful Counselor, the Counselor of all counselors, His name is Jesus. Jesus' way of being, understanding, and intervening in Mary's issues is the same way He intervenes in the lives of people today.

Women have suffered fear, helplessness, feelings of guilt, shame, low self-worth, and more as a result of reliving day-in and day-out marginalized, oppressed, and subjected to violence towards their psychological, emotional, and social functioning. Their cognitive processing and experiencing disturbances in thought, concentration, perceptions, and images results in significant distress while trying to live and not die. Demonic possession in that day, was considered a psychological and physical illness that overwhelmed and overpowered the person so that they in many cases had no control of their behavior or living. Today some might call it a mental illness, such as, schizophrenia, anxiety, major depressive disorder, and various personality disorders.

Just as in the days Jesus lived on this earth, women today experience these same symptoms that define posttraumatic stress disorder (PTSD).

Systematic racism that oppress the poor and powerless affect every system of societies and render its citizens exposed to traumatic events involving actual or perceived threats of death or serious injury. Survival responses are often confused and labeled as problem behavior, such as, angry Black women or men, hypervigilant, impulsive, careless, or avoidant. In reality, oppressed people struggle to breathe, to exhale, to live.

Jesus helped Mary move from subjugation to liberation; from shame to self-worth, from an unjust society to a beloved community where all are treated as equal; from judgment to forgiveness; and from demonic possession to healing and wholeness. Mary was transformed from death to life. She found meaning and purpose. She committed this newfound freedom to serving and taking up the mission to help liberate others. Jesus broke through many barriers that separated people because of class, gender, ethnicity, religion, and social economic status. Jesus brought community, friendship, fellowship, and a redemptive process designed to lift and restore women to their rightful position and purpose they were to enjoy in God's original creation. It was not just women that Jesus restored to health and well-being. He also restored sight to the blind, fed the hungry, spent time in the homes of the so called, "common people". Whatever the need, Jesus fulfilled it.

As a pastoral counselor, we should view the client's inner wisdom as an ally to help unravel the various reasons they may have lost their way from the sacred and to help them facilitate the connection back to their inner knowing and intuitive clarity (Johnson, 20130). Pastoral counselors can help clients navigate the pathways that are an appropriate fit for the problem, and to bring awareness to the possibility of the need for change. This change journey is embodied in the Serenity Prayer, written by Reinhold Niebuhr.

"God grant me the serenity to accept the things I cannot change, courage to change the things I can, and wisdom to know the difference."

Liberation of Meaning and Purpose

As I look back over my life and the journey I have traveled, I have learned many lessons. I remembered all my encounters with suffering, sorrow and the development of my scars. I have learned to embrace suffering and sorrow and allow them to teach me how to endure and accept my situation with joy and thankfulness. I learned there are some things I cannot change and then there are some things I can. I learned how to seek God's Word and believe that each scar had a meaning and purpose that I could not understand, but believed the bible scriptures, *that all things worked together for the good of those who love God and are the called according to His purpose* (Romans 8:28). I learned how to forgive those who hurt me and forgive myself for those that I hurt.

I learned that God sees me not as what I am today, but what He created me to be; created in His image and made for good. Every circumstance in life, no matter how crooked and distorted and ugly it appears to be, if it is reacted to in love and forgiveness and obedience to God's will, it can be transformed. Therefore, I like the fictional character introduced earlier, Much-Afraid (who was transformed to Grace and Glory), understood that God purposely allows us to be brought into contact with the bad and evil things that God wants to change (Hurnard, 2012). Perhaps that is the very reason why we are here in this world, where sin and sorrow and suffering and evil abound, so that we may let God teach us how to react to them; and that out of them we can create lovely qualities that live forever. That is the only satisfactory way of dealing with evil, not simply binding it so that it cannot work harm, but whenever possible overcoming it with good (Cooper,

2013, p. 216). When I am able to accept my sorrow and suffering with joy, and bear evil with love, I can join in partnership with God to overcome evil, sorrow, and the ugly things in the world. It is then I am transformed from Much-Afraid to Grace and Glory.

King David experienced challenges often. Yet, he had great faith. As a young Jewish boy, he grew up under the traditions of his family, serving God. He was a shepherd, the keeper of sheep. He was responsible for feeding the flock, but also ensuring their protection from lions, bears, and wolves. King David's faith was radical monotheism, belief in One True God. Like Rev. Dr. Martin Luther King, Gandhi, and Mother Teresa, King David's leadership was built on his pursuit of social truth that is justice. King David actualized the spirit of an inclusive and fulfilled human community. Even as a young boy, his family values and beliefs were shaped by the One True God who had proven His faithfulness by signs, wonders, and miracles in delivering his people, the Jews, from Egyptian slavery. His faith was exercised in the social, political, and economic areas of life as a Jew. That radical monotheistic faith drove King David to face a giant, Goliath. As we would say, King David brought five smooth stones to a sword fight. But he spoke his faith, he believed that His God would deliver him from the hands of Goliath and God did. David killed the giant because he believed His God was bigger and more powerful than Goliath.

People who come to counseling at times find their faith challenged because as defined, *faith is the substance of things hoped for, and the evidence of things not seen* (Hebrews 11:1). The problems they face are monumental, giants, as some call them. Their faith becomes challenged because things are not happening the way they want them to happen and when they want it to happen. Immediate results, no waiting for gratification and resolutions down the road. However, this was how King David's faith was tested and how he built a radical universal faith in God. David was a shepherd who protected sheep. His natural inclination was to protect the weak, those who could not protect themselves. He killed lions and bears to protect what was sacred to him. He volunteered to fight Goliath. The Jewish army was being taunted by the giant. The Jews saw this problem as unsurmountable. They were afraid. King David went into action to defend his people and to kill the giant who was also defaming the name of his God. In all the hardships and challenges King David faced he never wavered in his faith in God. God never failed him. The proof of God's faithfulness was demonstrated over and over again. The universality of all of God's creation is respected and cared for. We who are loved by God, will be cared for and protected.

When we face trouble or the loss of a loved one, we can feel like life no longer has meaning. Especially for couples who have been married for 50, 60, even 70 years. Their very identity can be wrapped-up in the identity of the spouse or significant other. This is an issue that will bring a client to counseling, searching for answers. So consumed with grief, their functioning in everyday life becomes impaired. They come to counseling angry at God but rationalizing they cannot hold the anger too long because they need to trust God to help them. Sometimes when God is needed the most, His presence cannot be felt. The feeling of loneliness becomes very real.

No two people will grieve alike. There are many grieving styles. Symptoms of confusion slowed thinking, sadness, meaninglessness, intense anguish, withdrawal, sleep and eating disturbances become very real challenges when working with clients and doing grief work. The survivor of the lost loved one may need help to get to the point of being able to integrate the loss of their loved one into their new life. The goal is to review the loss in therapy and resolve the unfinished business of the guilt, shame, or other emotional challenges felt surrounding whatever failure they think about their own behavior during the time their loved was alive. Clients have said it was their failure of faith to believe in the miracle of healing the loved one desired. People can become confused and experience conflict in their relationship with God.

Watching a loved one suffer in a long-term illness is painful, hard, and physically and emotionally draining. Being angry with God but needing God to help get through the pain can be terrifying for them. Your desire is for the loved one to no longer be in pain, nevertheless, a feeling of guilt and shame for wanting God to relieve them from their suffering. Ultimately, that would mean death. No one wishes their loved one to die, that would be an awful thing to even think about.

My pastoral perspective and spiritual assessment for such a client is to assess their spiritual and faith formation. How were they taught at early stages of life and about their Christian faith traditions? Unguided in the Christian faith by parents who are not religious or spiritual, or not connected with a Christian faith community, one's faith may never fully develop with a strong foundation. Faith formation is developed and grown by testing of trials, experiences, both good and challenging. A person can become enmeshed into the identity of another because they depend totally on others for everything. In some marriages, the husband takes care of everything. It is then the realization comes that work is needed to build one's own spirituality faith. Can you identify with this statement, "My conscience is responsive to social evils that are among the root causes of the pain and brokenness of individuals?" Are you able to connect with the biopsychosocial and epigenetic (nature/nurture) view of being root causes of pain and brokenness in individuals? It can give insight into faith development concerning how a person can view God, spirituality and the connectedness of all things being interrelated.

This level of faith development is known as Fowler's Stage 2 – Mythic-Literal Faith and Piaget's Concrete Operational Stage. Piaget's theory states that children go through four stages of cognitive development as they actively construct their understanding of the world, namely organization and adaptation. The Concrete Operational Stage is where children can perform operations that involve objects, and they can reason logically when the reasoning can be applied to specific or concrete examples. They cannot imagine the steps or thinking that is too abstract at this stage of development (Santrock, 2011, p. 25). Fowler's Mythic-Literal faith works very hard and effectively at sorting out the real from the make-believe. Within the range of his or her ability to investigate and test, children will insist on demonstration or proof for claims of facts. Pertaining to faith, the Mythic-Literal stage brings the ability to bind experiences into meaning through the medium of stories. The stories are of great adventures – true or realistically fictional, they appeal because of their inherent interest, and they become the media for extension of their experience and understanding in life (Fowler, 1981, p. 136).

However, in the Formal Operational Stage, a child reasons in more abstract, idealistic, and logical ways. This stage allows the faith development to take stories, reflect upon them, and communicate their meanings by way of more abstract and general statements. If you do not have the ability to demonstrate the understanding of the story of Moses and the parting of the Red Sea, as a miracle; your belief would say, one day I will look-up and see my loved one come through the door, even though you know the loved one has died. It means your faith has not been crystalized to believe in and understand how to apply greater meaning and understanding of the sacred texts to life's experiences. Rather, the belief becomes more literal in meaning. One can be drawn to the word, but never understand the deeper meaning of what the scriptures are saying in reference to life experiences.

When this becomes an issue in counseling for a client, it becomes a countertransference issue for me. I am reminded of the story in the bible where an Ethiopian eunuch was sitting in a chariot reading the scriptures. Phillip, a disciple of Christ, by the Holy Spirit, was told to go over to the chariot. He asked the Ethiopian if he understood what he was reading. The Ethiopian said to Phillip, "how can I understand when there is no one to guide me?" The Ethiopian asked Phillip to sit with him. The Ethiopian Eunuch was reading from Isaiah 53:7-8, about Jesus (Acts 8:26-40). Right there, Phillip preached Jesus to him. Salvation, faith in Jesus Christ, came to the house of the Ethiopian Eunuch that day and he was baptized. Phillip said, "if you believe with all your heart...and make the confession that Jesus Christ is the Son of God...you may be saved and baptized." My countertransference was what Phillip did with the Ethiopian eunuch; preaching the gospel of Jesus. I would have done it with the client, right then and right now. However, because of my therapist/client relationship and the ethical standards that prohibits proselytizing, I could not act on that opportunity.

What do you do when experiencing the pain of impending loss of a loved one and you have prayed, and God has not answered your prayer? What if God does not give you the miracle of healing? Many trying to cope with the loved one's death, will go walking early in the morning to pray. It is a time to gather strength to make it through the day. My pastoral perspective would be to challenge you to be more open and aware of your surroundings, to take in the beauty of things that are around you, and to be more open to exploration and meaning of the things you see.

Your prognosis can be very good if you are open to rebuilding a support network of family, friends, and a faith community. If you are open to grief counseling, be very cooperative in doing homework assignments by practicing relaxation exercises and gaining insight on your own strengths. Open up your awareness and experience in building and strengthening your spirituality, not only in the scriptures, but in the beauty of nature and the extraordinary interrelatedness of your surroundings.

I came to the realization that many of my issues were because of oppression, from ideological thoughts and practices of worldview social systems, and a culture of patriarchal racial superiority in White America. Two life changing moments occurred because of two classes I took in Pastoral Counseling and Christian Ethics while matriculating at

Howard University School of Divinity (HUSD). The first book, *Moving From Shame to Self-Worth*, by Edward P. Wimberly, shaped my new theology of Jesus' mission in the world to bring about social change in the world that was built on classism, sexism, racism, gender biases and differences; to a more egalitarian world where there were no class stratified shame-based societies. In the days of class stratification systems, a person's worth was value-laden, based on honor and shame. There were those who were highly valued and then there were those who were not. Those considered unworthy were the marginalized and disenfranchised, who were the members of the lower classes, the sick, and the poor. To the extent that they internalized their station in life, they viewed themselves as worthless and valueless (Wimberly, 1999). Jesus was a political figure during his time; grasping that, I then understood the only way of change was not only through social activism, but also through coming to terms with the oppressive forms of social evil that are part of the world in which I live. Jesus experienced this same shame and oppression as told in his life story.

The second life changing moment was a Social Ethics class also taken at HUSD, and it was through a book called, *Kingdom Ethics*, by Glen H. Stassen and David P. Gushee. This book helped to shape my radical but practical way of living and thinking. I call it cognitive behavioral therapy that changed how I understood and behaved toward the Christian ethos that Jesus established and taught surrounding justice, mercy, love, truth, and interpersonal relationships. There are fourteen transforming initiatives that were taken from Jesus' *Sermon on the Mount* that helped to transform radical thinking of opposites in taking the "below" way as opposed to the "above" way, the way of humility. Thus, it caused less of an agonizing struggle between power desired and power obtained (Stassen & Gushee, 1999, pp. 125-145).

This way of being, understanding and intervening was the pathway that helped move me toward the development of my foundation of theory and practice in becoming a pastoral counselor. These were the formative years of my desire for helping relationships to improve the quality of life, fight against social injustices, prejudices, gender biases, classism, sexism, and racial discrimination. I was highly effective and successful in social activism around raising the level of awareness and understanding the dynamics of domestic violence and intimate partner violence. I often listen to lifestyle stories of individuals trying to reconcile their pasts of abuse, shame, and guilt, and how their faith, values, beliefs, and spirituality helped or hindered their healing and recovery.

Chapter II – Theoretical Approach

The foundation of desiring to help others can be discovered through our own profound and personal life experiences. As an African American female, I often wonder why I have always had a desire to help others make their lives better. Pain and suffering have been an intricate part of my life. My personal life experiences are eyewitness testimonies of the political ideologies of the country in which I was born. As a developing counselor, my ideology in practice of a helping relationship is best captured through Adler's Individual Psychology, Feminism and Feminist Thought and Therapy, and Black Feminist Thought.

My theological thought of Liberation Theology undergirds my clinical theories and spotlights how and why I have been successful thus far in my clinical internship of helping clients with interventions that have caused growth where they have integrated the tools and language of their healing.

Foundation of Theory

When I first entered the pastoral program in 2011, my undergraduate work in psychology had laid a foundation of psychodynamic theory as the best theory to explain my scars. However, I gained more knowledge and new insights about my scars. I built altars of sacrifice, giving the hurts and pains over to God, and allowing the pain and hurt to be burnt up. I made conscious and intentional decisions to forgive and allow God to bring healing to my soul and letting love's seed grow. This love was not only love for others, but also love for me.

My soul still gets restless from the unanswered questions of the ups and downs of life's circumstances and how they relate to my life purpose. Webster's Dictionary defines soul as "an entity without material reality, regarded as the spiritual part of a person". The soul is the deep spiritual and emotional quality of Black Americans. The spirit is regarded as religion, and sacred; life, will, and thought. As an African American female, I define my soul as the seat of my consciousness, intentions, motivations, and thoughts. It is the turmoil of my soul that forces me to wrestle with the ongoing struggles of reconciling me to the outer forces of my environment and with those who help to make my life plan a reality. The strength of my spirit grounds my soul and establishes my emotions to the truth and reality of my existence along with the polarities of life that can either oppress me or elevate me. Memories and experiences also helped to shape my emotions (Mairet, 1999).

However, memories and experiences are more forms of oppression in the economic, political, social, and religious areas that make up my life as an African American woman in mainstream America. Economic, because no matter how far I have advanced up the corporate ladder, my pay scale has not reached that of the so-called, "good old boy network" of the white male worker. I know very well of political oppression, because all my efforts to fight for equal rights and social justice for women and men who are victims of domestic violence have been met with failing laws that were written to protect and preserve life; but have been met with hardened hearts of judges, unknowledgeable lawyers, and a society that blames the victim for his/her abuse. Women have been killed because of lack of enforced laws that protect victims of abuse from their perpetrator. Judges have denied orders of protection that could have kept women safe from abuse. I have spoken on Capitol Hill, lobbying for laws and victims' rights.

Equality and social acceptance of under-privileged children in the public education system have been challenged with a lack of understanding of the issues at-risk children experience in their day-to-day existence. The absence of empathy for children, who through no fault of their own, are products of faulty social and educational systems that have been built on a foundation of suppressing Black thinkers and the Black intellectually astute (Collins, 2000).

The halls of academia are filled with discriminatory practices making access to knowledge to the lower classes unattainable due to economic disparities. The halls of our religious institutions and places of worship while included in this disparity, are the last place I expected to find oppression and discrimination at astronomical proportions. How did I think that the very fabric of American society and patriarchal domination would not cross the boundaries of religious thought and practice?

Personal Counseling Theory Development

I have shared earlier how my life story has shaped my worldview and how I view my life span development that can be explained by Mary Ainsworth's attachment theory in my formative years by an emotionally absent parent. My cognitive development I believe can be described by Albert Bandura's Social Cognitive Theory. This theory holds to the notion that behavior, environment, and cognition are the key factors in development. Albert Bandura, an American psychologist, emphasizes that our process of knowing, perception, and knowledge have important links with the environment and behavior such that his early research program focused heavily on observational learning, called imitation or modeling. This learning occurs through observing what others do (Santrock, 2011, p. 27). I observed and learned from others that which I wanted to do. It served me for a while, but not to the degree that financial prosperity, social prowess, and political power enabled me to sustain any ground gained for too long.

My goal was to pursue higher education to combat the disparities that people experienced and to rid myself of the ignorance and the helplessness I felt because I knew so little about the realities of life and the social systems in which I lived. My plan was to obtain my undergraduate degree in Business Management to help level the playing field in my economic disparity. But after several years of working in ministry and ministering to women, men, and children around their hurts, pains, and crises in life, I changed my major to Psychology. I wanted to know about the inner workings of the mind and how thought and thinking along with experiences shaped our personalities and helped us to heal and change our social and personal perspectives, or not.

Individual Psychology, Feminism, Feminist Thought and Therapy, and Black Feminist Thought are the approaches to helping relationships that most closely tell my story. I see my story on the pages of Patricia Hill Collin's (2000) book, *Black Feminist Thought*, in labor discriminatory practices, being overlooked for promotions while being well qualified to do the job but given to a male counterpart who I helped to make successful. I see my story on the pages of E.P. Wimberly's book, *Moving from Shame to Self-Worth*, as I bore the shame and guilt as damaged goods because of rape and molestation in my childhood and young adult years. I see the stories of my parishioners who struggle to make their lives meaningful, but because of economic disparities and excessive costs of housing are forced to live on the streets of America. I see senior citizens, who have helped to build America and its prosperity, and now they watch the rich get richer, and they struggle with pennies from social security checks that barely pay their living expenses. My soul shares in the struggle daily with others like myself who have a life plan of meaning, purpose, health, and a good life, where all our needs are met, work-life, social relationships, and personal intimate relationships are all congruent. My perfect world is there are no classes defined by inferiority and superiority; a world where my soul is healed and at peace with God and with others. The scars I carry, and those others carry, are the roadmaps to where we have been.

I will continue to grow as I experience working with families globally of diverse populations to help them realize their life plans and goals. Specifically, working with African American youth who will grow and excel in their development of Black critical thinking, art, music, poetry, technology, or whatever their minds can conceive, that will make the world a better place to live. To be a part of shaping a new world by entering into the worldview of others and helping to liberate them from the oppressive forces of the dysfunctional world system in which we live today, is my life goal.

Approaches to Helping Relationships

Ways of Understanding. I see my soul and my spirit in battle one with the other. I am trying to support a good life, and a healthy self portrait of a life plan that is served with equal rights, mercy, and justice. I envision an egalitarian world that is free from the shame of being classified as "below" and not "above" (Mairet, 1999, pg. 31). Patricia Hill Collins (2000) in her book, *Black Feminist Thought* writes to help empower African American women. I knew that "when an individual

Black woman's consciousness concerning how she understands her everyday life undergoes change, she can become empowered." Such consciousness may stimulate her to embark on a path of personal freedom, even if it exists initially primarily in her own mind. If she is lucky enough to meet others who are undergoing similar journeys, she and they can change the world around them. If ideas, knowledge, and consciousness can have such an impact on individual Black women, what effect might they have on Black women as a group.?

Black feminist thought is concerned with racial discrimination, gender biases, and gender stereotyping that shape American thinking toward women in general and African American women specifically. However, African American feminist thought challenges the very core of ideologies, practices, and thoughts that subjugate African American women and other women of color living in a white, male dominated society (Collins, 2000, pp. 6-8). Feminist therapy and Adlerian Counseling for the individual examines the impact of how social, political, economic, and religious issues shape the conscientiousness of an individual's worldviews and self-existence through personal narrative and lifestyle stories respectively. Adler, like many of the theorists of feminist thought and therapy, was an advocate of justice issues and an advocate of women's rights (Sicking, 2011). Socialization into the family, community, and the world at-large play an important role in identity and development of the individual (Mairet, 1999).

Childhood and adult experiences shape personality and influence behavior surrounding social interactions, work, and interpersonal relationships. These three areas are critical lifestyle development tasks that Adlerian views as shaping the whole person (Sicking, 2011). Trouble or crisis in any one of these areas challenge the essence of what Adler calls the "soul" (Mairet, 1999, p. 10). The soul shapes the conscious and unconscious thoughts, memories, and emotions in response to all lived experiences (Mairet, 1999). All activities of the soul are drawn together into the service of the individual, (Mairet, 1999). Ways of being and understanding in therapy is to enter the world of others by identifying with their ideas, difficulties, efforts, and joys. Understanding the thoughts and ideas of others can bring empathy to the relationship to encourage change, rather than label and dissect behaviors or thoughts as psychosis, but rather see and understand that they are survival strategies toward oppressive and/or marginalized tactics used to further patriarchal dominance and agendas (Collins, 2000).

In *ABC of Adler's Psychology* (Mairet, 1999), Dr. Adler is quoted, *"No psychic phenomenon can be grasped and understood unless it is regarded as the preparation of an integrated life plan and some goal."* The task is to understand all the movements and emotional phases of an individual, to get to the picture of an integrated life plan and a final goal." (Mairet, 1999, p. 27). The life plan is the driving force behind all our thoughts and actions. The living experience becomes the "as if" (p. 29), the life plan is the ideal of who we are within our social sphere of existence. As such, we measure the life plan next to our three critical life tasks of community and/or social relations, satisfaction in work accomplishments, and intimate or social relationships (i.e., marriage, boyfriend/girlfriend) to determine healthiness and a good life. Our inability to see our life plan as congruent to our actualized experiences can become overwhelming to the coping strategies, we have established to survive day to day. Challenge to our ideal life plan, challenges the totality of our very existence, and thus causes dysfunction and stress, and the individual becomes a client because of the inability to cope (Mairet, 1999).

In therapy, the client comes face to face with the lived experiences of living in a world that promotes inferiority and superiority, and it has taken a toll on the psychological, physical, emotional, and spiritual prowess of self-existence. The reality of oppression, discrimination, and segregation have shattered the ideal life plan. All efforts have been their own human strivings to make sense of his/her existence and the good life to which they have struggled to find. The social pressures, stereotypes, and biases continue to dominate societal norms that promote "above" or "below" class stratifications. The polarities to which human existence ascribe between male and female, black and white, perpetuate superiority versus inferiority complexes and further exacerbates societal ine-qualities and domination of some over others. Thus, a vicious cycle of striving to overcome inferiority by devising an ideal life plan is revealed as futile. Adler likens this to the biological principal when injury is done to one part of the body; it over-compensates or develops new parts to replace that part that is injured. (Mairet, 1999, pp. 15-23). "Man (humanity) is in the critical predicament of having to save his own being by the creation of the supra-biological organism, human society." (Mairet, 1999, p. 23)

The reality of oppression, discrimination, and abuse has shattered many ideal life plans. All efforts have been made by their own human strivings to make sense of their existence and the good life to which they have struggled to ascertain. Their realities were the social pressures, stereotypes, and biases that continue to dominate societal norms that promote the "above" and "below" class stratifications in the places in which they are forced to live. Comparatively, sometimes spirituality and religious beliefs become a roadblock; while my spirituality served as a resource.

Ways of Being and Intervening. Feminist thought purports women can tell their stories and should be given the opportunity to tell of their experiences as viewed through their own lens. Each person's experience is different and is shaped by a worldview that has originated out of their personal social experience and development. The context in which women experience oppression are reframed to experiences of role conflict, coping strategies for surviving oppression, and are the result of socialization and labeling for deviation from traditional gender roles (Evans, Kincade, Marbley, & Seem, 2005, p. 272). Social activism is another form of intervention that gives rise to clients' empowerment over their oppression. In Black feminist thought, the use of music, poetry, essays, and other forms of writing have been encouraged to produce social thought to oppose oppression. (Collins, 2000, p. 9)

I have found the intervention strategies of Adlerian Counseling are remarkably similar to that of the feminist thought and can work together in helping relationships with clients. Namely, telling of life plan or life-style stories. The goal is to get to a complete portrait of personality.

The outcome is a breakdown, a release from reality, a psychopathology to escape reality of the ideal life goal or plan, self-elevation, from inferiority to superiority, when we fail. The purpose of individual psychology, in so doing, will help to expose the life plan or goal when it threatens the conscious purpose and realization of actualization of the individual. (Mairet, 1999).

Encouragement and empathy are vital to helping to promote the desire to change while eradicating misconceptions and reshaping thought and behavior. These means of intervention foster a collaborative partnership of respect and trust between client and therapist (Corey, 2009).

The use of spiritual beliefs and values also assist in the helping relationship. The use of scriptures and religious experience has been a source of encouragement. Some transparency of therapist experience has also fostered trust and respect with the client. Long term interventions are through continued education of women. Also, clients who find their voice to tell of their narrative stories in society, work toward fighting social injustice to bring about social change. In Christian theology, Jesus taught that participation in God's

81

reign requires the disciplined practices of a Christ-following countercultural community that obeys God by publicly engaging in working for justice and refusing to trust in the world's powers and authorities (Stassen & Gushee, 2003).

My way of intervening with some clients is using the eclectic approach, using Adlerian Brief Therapy which is defined as intervention that is short termed, purposeful, direct, and concise (Corey, 2009, p.54), and based on the Growth Model. The Feminist Model can also be used to help narrate personal stories through subjective interviewing; and an informal lifestyle assessment to gain an understanding of worldview, cultural viewing of self, others, and the world. In addition, it can help to move towards gaining personal power. As an Adlerian and Feminist practitioner, I am not bound to follow a specific set of techniques or procedures but could apply techniques that are most appropriate for the client. The techniques used with the client can include empathic attending (listening), encouragement, laughter, suggesting, homework assignments, and summarizing. In solidifying the second part of the Dual Process Model of Grief, in the reorientation process, the goal is to help the client to successful Identity

Achievement, reach their fullest potential, and create a new lifestyle without the loss loved one.

My way of being with all clients is based on mutual respect and a collaborative partnership where we, client and therapist, are active parties in a relationship of equality (Corey, 2009, p. 53). Every aspect of the client's actions is interpreted by helping him or her gain insight, meaning, and connections between past, present, and future strivings. Gerald Corey (2009) suggests that initial trust and rapport, and sustained attention on the quality of the therapeutic relationship make the challenging work of changing one's style of living a possibility.

Heredity and environment play an important role in human development and also influence the biological development in brain development that predisposes individuals to limited cognitive and social development processes that can cause dysfunction in current living and stagnation and/or despair in later life. The following are goals a client and therapist can set together. This is an example of a client who desires to rebuild their life after losing a loved one.

Communications. Client describes themself as shy and an introvert. The desire is to be able to be more outgoing and talk with others. It is also a desire to learn how to overcome shyness.

Cognitive Therapy- Technique: Stress positive capacities. Reframe thinking of negative beliefs to more positive frames of reference. Identify distorted thinking and misperceptions. Changing language and self-talk. Use of laughter as a way of reducing stress and to help cope and survive this stressful lifestyle that has been lived.

Overcome sadness. Interrupt the ruminations and memories of a deceased loved one by using relaxation exercises, encouragement to face life tasks, learn to sit with grief, and not dismiss it. Release of guilt and weight that is being carried surrounding a lack of faith.

Develop Social Support Network. Without a support system, a client's prognosis would be poor. Re-engaging in a faith community and with friends can give the encouragement needed and also help to build self-esteem because of the care and nurture relationships can provide.

Build Self-Esteem. Recall early recollections that have shaped worldview and self- portrait. Explore memories, impressions, and conclusions that have been formed around how self, other people, and the world is seen.

What conclusions have been formed about life based on thought patterns?

The Adlerian Brief Therapy Model can be applied to help move a client to establishing an identity that does not imitate or model others but establishes and empowers them to be comfortable with who they are becoming. Clients come to counseling hopeless, despondent, and broken. Their whole life and identity have been wrapped up in another's identity for years. I did not believe that in ten sessions a life could be turned around. However, I attribute this work to God's intervention and answered prayers that I prayed before sessions. My willingness to be open to allow the Spirit of God to use me as an instrument to help facilitate healing leaves me in awe.

In relaxation exercises, the client's catharsis, release of the emotional pain and tensions, can come through a guided full body relaxation exercise. The exercise asks the client to find a special place that is quiet, safe, and peaceful in the mind and to allow each part of their body to relax. They are to release anything that is disturbing their ability to relax. After the exercise, the client describes their experience.

One observation shared was, "My arms are empty, I feel relief like I let something go, I feel relieved - feel like I can go to sleep now. I could sleep before, but not peaceful. I feel completely relaxed with no resistance. The tightening of my shoulders and arms, that are usually tense, I do not feel anymore. The tension in my shoulders I do not feel anymore."

In exploring the meaning with the client, they were letting go of the guilt they were feeling about a loved one's death. The death was not anything they could control. Their arms were carrying the burden of guilt they had felt.

The client continues to use the tools they acquired in counseling. They often use this exercise at home, going to a special place that brings peace, quiet, and solitude where rest can be found. The gain of new hope and faith is formed assuring that the sadness of losing the loved one would pass and something good would come out of it all. The termination session can be initiated by the client. They leave counseling with many experiences since their first session of learning how to navigate life on their own. They know they are different from the first day of counseling and they will continue to grow and get better. Now, spirituality has become a resource for them as they continue to grow and foster the curiosity and understanding of scriptures. They are now able to integrate the tools and language of the clinical acumen. I understand from my clinical supervisor, "this is what every clinician long to hear and see." The client leaves counseling with identity achievement, empowered, and equipped to take on life on their own terms.

Strengths and Limitations

In helping relationships, Adler's Individual Psychology, Feminism and Feminist Thought, and Black Feminist Thought all bring the goal of social justice for the individual in their lived experiences, but also to bring about social change within their communities and world at-large. They promote eradication of gender bias, stereotyping of any kind with any race or culture, and can use other techniques from other counseling theories. They share ways of being and intervening with other therapy theories whose focus require specific, necessary and sufficient conditions for healing, (i.e., congruence, empathy, authenticity) (Sicking, 2011). Thought and practice can be used with a variety of clients across diverse populations (Corey, 2009). Since humans are social beings, the strength of its practice and philosophy engages ways of living healthy in society even though there are oppositional and oppressive practices that are engrained in the societal norms.

The strength of the relationship between client and therapist has potential for a stronger bond of respect and trust when labeling and diagnosing are not used to explain frame of reference for lived experiences. The use of engaging the client in the use of spiritual beliefs, values, and experiences also bring strength to understanding the client as a whole person engaging every aspect of their existence.

Limitations of Adlerian concepts and approaches are not precisely defined and are difficult to confirm through empirical studies. Many of the tenets are said to be oversimplified, when human functioning is very complex (Corey, 2009). Even though Adlerian theory does support negating gender bias, it still does discriminate in some instances of male and female roles (Mairet, 1999). Feminism and feminist thought have few neutral stances concerning gender issues and social change and social structures at-large. The voice of feminist thought can range from mild to very radical in their commitment to bring about social justice and to fight against social injustice to the oppressed (Evans et al., 2005). It is believed that therapists may potentially impose their own views and beliefs that would be counter to cultural traditions and norms Corey, 2009).

Unfortunately, in earlier works with feminism and feminist thought, the foundation of theory was written by white middle-class women. White feminists have resisted embracing their Black feminist colleagues which has had a pronounced influence on feminist theory (Collins, 1999, p. 5).

Gender bias within gender and race remain a critical issue in suppression of the Black voice. Embedded in European culture and other non-black traditions are thoughts of super self- ideals, of self-grandeur and intellect that have created a psychosis of alienation from one's own people and Black thought. The exclusion of Black feminist theorists remains a long-standing problem in hearing the voice of the oppressed in mainstream political, economic, and social arenas. Even though Black feminists have made strides in being included, oppression is more covert than overt. Black literary works and texts have been used in the classrooms, but the presence of the Black author is not. Suppression of the Black voice still brings limitations to access to critical areas in educational, political, economic, and social areas that keep the stereotypical images and ideas before the eye and minds of non-white and the popular culture, to protect white male interests and worldviews (Collins, 1999, p. 3).

Chapter III Critique and Future Plans

A life message is a signpost that reveals to others who they really are and speaks to their meaning and purpose in life, so are my scars. I see my scars as the messages that are the sum of my life experiences that have grounded me in understanding of God's love. I have taken to heart and affirm that my focus as a pastoral counselor has been shaped by the unique ways my journey of experiences has defined how I have access to life-affirming beliefs and practices. But the unifying idea that embracing a loving and compassionate heart allows people to make decisions based on joy and abundance instead of fear and scarcity, choose to live in liberation and not in pain and suffering. I have shared my scars, and as you have come to understand, there are different types of pain. In our culture today, we look at pain as completely negative and most of us try to avoid pain and suffering at all costs. However, when we can look at pain from God's perspective, we can see that it is supposed to mean, "Comfort is on the way" (Moon & Moon, 2007, p. 24). As children we learn early that pain is something that is to be feared and avoided. We withdraw from things or people that hurt or betray us. As a result, we carry these ideals into adulthood and expend a lot of energy trying to avoid pain; which causes us a lot of relational problems (Moon & Moon, pp. 24-25).

God's way includes us sitting with another in their pain without trying to fix them, interceding in prayer for them, and putting an end to feeling another's feelings for them. These options can be difficult and will bring pain to the helper (Moon & Moon, 2007, p. 24). As a pastoral counselor, I can view pain differently realizing that scars are a part of life, and they show what you've been through. It is through painful lessons that I have grown the most. *"Now no chastening seems to be joyful for the present, but painful; nevertheless, afterwards it yields the peaceable fruit of righteousness to those who have been trained by it"* (Hebrews 12:15).

Learning to accept, or embrace with joy, all God allows to happen to us is a critical lesson that ushers us into maturity (Cooper, 2013, p. 220). The bible is full of examples and stories of what can happen when we accept what God has allowed in our lives and when we faithfully continue to serve the Lord.

The ultimate meaning of my life and purpose is embodied in the story of God's love for humanity. Jesus chose the path of suffering and carrying the scars on His back as He journeyed down the road to Golgotha. To love means to put oneself under the power of the loved one and to become very vulnerable to pain (Hurnard, 2012). This is not how God defines love. Nothing is too much, or too unbearable when true love exists. Our finite minds cannot understand the love God has for us, and as a result we live way beneath the privileges and freedoms we have in relationship with God. This is the limitation I see in this metaphor; we come to know and understand our story and learn to love as we know it. Yet will we give our lives willingly for the cause of love for another? Love is a universal emotion that is available to be experienced by all of humanity, but have we experienced the agape love that God has for us and desires we have for each other?

The seed of love has been planted in our hearts and the seed will grow as we follow our purpose and make meaning out of our lives in relation to God, with one another, oneself, and with all creation (Hurnard, 2012). This is done as we continue to pursue learning, being exposed to other cultures through travel, practicing self-care, continuing to build and strengthen our inner life, setting personal and ethical boundaries, taking time for enjoyment, laughter, and fun. Most importantly, we create a sacred space with God and spend quality time there often. When you arrive at your destiny, "love will not concern itself with pain" (Hurnard, 2012, p. 9). True love will meet you there. This is the hope I hold as a pastoral counselor for my clients.

Skills, Strengths, and Limitations

In my earlier job I participated in a program called Basic Leadership Development. We were charged to complete an assessment of our strengths with the Strength Finders 2.0 (Rath, 2007). Rath (2007) says, *"people who focus on their strengths are six times as likely to be engaged in their jobs and more than three times as likely to report having an excellent quality of life in general."* He also believes that more people spend countless hours focusing in on their weaknesses versus their strengths. In assessing and applying that statement to me, he is correct. In completing the assessment, it yielded my top five strengths as learner, connectedness, input, intellection, and harmony. These strengths align and undergird other tests and assessments I have taken as part of my development and education as a pastoral counselor. The psychological assessments I have taken accurately assessed and helped me to understand my intra-psychic processes. I had to choose to either build resilience or succumb to the horror of my experiences. I was driven to survive and fulfill my life goals. The Christian values and beliefs that I was taught as a child have grown from infantile faith that depended upon my caregivers (Fowler, 1981) to a more universal faith that is inclusive of all that God has created. As a result, I am prepared to support the growth and development of the next generation.

As an African American woman, I believe I have the DNA of my ancestors to survive the dangers, hurt, suffering, and pain that have been part and parcel to our history as a people. Spirituality and religion have always been a part of my cultural heritage. My father as my attachment figure supplied the love, nurturing and example of what God, my Heavenly Father, was to us as a family. Despite his challenges, he worked very hard to support his family.

As an adult child of a parent that had challenges with alcohol (ACOA), I wanted to understand how growing up in a dysfunctional environment influenced my development. An article by Hall and Webster (2007), "Risk Factors Among Adult Children of Alcoholics", gave me insight on some of the personality traits that I could identify within myself: 1) don't talk about family problems, 2) it is not appropriate to express feelings openly, 3) nothing is ever good enough and you are still expected to strive for unobtainable perfection, 4) you have to work for the benefit of others and you can't be selfish, 5) limit communications, 6) at all cost avoid conflict, and 7) there is no room for play..

Other assessment results defined me as a thinker. My internal world of creative thoughts and plans helped me to become successful and provide a better life for myself. I accomplished my success through hard work, determination, sticking to commitments and tasks until completed and creative problem solving. I learned how to become the caretaker in the family for my younger sisters and to be helpful to my mother. With eight siblings, I could not compete being the middle child. There was always someone older who could pull the authority card, or someone younger who could pull the sympathy card.

While everything external to my existence appeared threatening and dangerous, I had my inner world of peace and calm. What I lacked in interpersonal relationships, I gained in achievement, affiliations, and intellectual stimulation. I have a love for learning, discovering new things, and being able to share my newfound discoveries with others. I enjoy the beauty of a sunrise or a sunset and being alone by the water, watching the waves flow in and out.

Having lived in a home where the use of alcohol existed, being sexually assaulted, domestic violence in my marriage, and going through religious crises, I can identify with chaos. Nevertheless, I find solitude and peace when I withdraw from everything and everybody and have that alone time with just me and God. This is how I replenish my strength, my coping ability, and build resilience. I understand the high need for order in my life.

I have better psychosocial outcomes in my life because of my universal faith and spiritual wholeness. I have invested and entrusted my life to the God of my understanding. Life experiences and the love of God have given me an appreciation and understanding of greater life purposes. Moving beyond the acts of harm and forgiving, I find meaning of a greater good for all people. This is how I have psychologically matured in my faith. Prayer, meditation, and the study of the Word of God connect me with the faith community for a shared purpose of working toward a greater good for all humankind. As I have heard some people say, "God never wastes a hurt" and neither have I. This way of being informs my therapeutic alliance and clinical acumen in my way of understanding and intervening with my clients.

Being highly agreeable and displaying significant openness made me a great candidate for therapy. In a therapeutic relationship, the client should establish trust, authenticity, and be compliant to the process of counseling. Therapy has been a constant in my life to help me check myself when things don't always go right. The psychological assessments gave insight to the psychological necessity of being able to help see myself in a broader perspective, and thus give credibility to testing and assessment as a clinical tool to help my prospective clients. As a pastoral counselor, the Five Factor Model and ASPIRES are comprehensive models that have guided and informed me in using an eclectic theoretical model of intervention and ways of being with my clients. The tools that I have been given have helped me to be effective in helping to support experiences of healing and wholeness to people who have been challenged and broken by life experiences and events.

My pains, hurts, and struggles have been turned to triumphs as I have used my trials and adversity in life to help others who have, are, or will go through some of the same pains I have conquered. This is conducted through Isaac Ministries, Inc., an international non-profit 501(c) 3 organization of which I am the founder and president. This organization ministers to the needs of at-risk children, adolescents, and their families. It provides advocacy and training to domestic violence victims and others interested in learning about the dynamics of domestic violence. The STRONG test accurately showed my occupational themes of Social-Conventional and Enterprising (e.g., providing service to others, often in large organizations, religious activities, social service, teaching, public speaking, and office services).

I did not find any areas lacking in any of the assessments and reports. In a stability profile assessment, research suggests that my personality profile is likely to be stable throughout adulthood. It will also serve as a fair guide even in old age, barring any major catastrophic incidences. As I move toward the last stage of Erick Ericson's Stages of Development, which is the 60 plus years, Integrity, I hope to accomplish building and preparing future generations in a more just world of human existence and tolerance.

Future Plans

I thought I would continue my education by pursuing higher education of a doctoral program. I wanted to further develop my education and skills to bring about good for the world through research; especially, for African Americans. Great disparities exist where mental health research is addressing the racial inequalities, injustices, and violence that inform psychological and emotional well-being of African American. Even as I rewrite and edit this book, it has changed a lot since 2016 when my plan consisted of publishing this book, pursuing my licensing for a pastoral counselor, and continuing on for my doctoral degree. My father transitioned to be with the Lord on my graduation day, right after receiving my graduate degree. I was devastated and found myself in an unimaginable dark night of the soul for three years.

During those three years, I found myself "homeless", even though I was not out on the street. However, ever since I left home at 18 years old, I always had my own place to call home. I lost my car, my dignity, and my life as I knew it. Those dark years were definitely trying to take me out of God's plan for my life. I desperately tried to hold on to my faith, but it was sure enough spiritual warfare at its best. And it all began with losing the one person in the world that was most dear to me. One thing my father left me was Proverbs 3:5-6, *"Trust in the Lord with all your heart and lean not to your understanding. In all your ways acknowledge God, and He will direct your path."*

For three years I lived in an apartment with no furniture. I slept on the floor on a makeshift mat for a bed. This was a time that I needed God more than ever before. I found myself in the circumstances that bring people to counseling. I am an adamant advocate to recommend counseling. But that time, counseling was not the way the Lord led me. I had to totally trust and depend on Him. All through those years, God never failed me. I learned obedience. I learned discipline. I learned that kind of radical faith that comes only through trials and warfare. I drew closer to God through prayer and worship.

Going into the third year, I moved to the third place that I would live for the next three years and counting. I must say, it was always in my heart, wondering; God what is it you want me to do now? One morning, God spoke. He told me it was time to go back for my license. Mind you, I have now felt some restoration, sleeping in a new bed, furniture in my home, higher salary paying job, able to pay my bills, and a car. I always say that God has a sense of humor. I said to God, "It has been three years since I graduated. I haven't picked up a book, studied anything I learned, how am I going to pass a test for licensing?" My heart was pounding because I knew it was God speaking. I couldn't write it off and say, "Oh, it is just my imagination or my own inner voice." Tears began to flow, and fear was creeping in fast. Again, God spoke, "it is already done in heaven, now make it manifest on earth." Crocodile tears were flowing, and I began worshiping. I began to study again, and I couldn't remember anything. But I kept believing and praying. Finally, I scheduled time to take the test. I was terrified, but I kept believing God's word to me. On December 2, 2019. I sat for the NCE exam and passed. Right in that office when I received my test score, I hollered, "Thank you Jesus!"

The amazing thing was, everything I studied, was not on the test (at least in the format that I would remember studying). I went to my car, cried, and praised, and worshiped; thanking God for His faithfulness. As of January 2020, I am a Licensed Graduate Professional Counselor, working in an organization that serve victims of crime and others in need of mental health services. God fulfilled His Word, all I had to do was be obedient. God's Providence and Sovereignty will blow your mind. Who would have thought in the next three months, March 2020 we would be in the midst of a global pandemic? The need for mental health services, pastoral counsel is great. Millions of people have died, millions are sick, thousands have lost their jobs, stress and hopelessness is at an all-time high. Medical workers have committed suicide, and the world as we knew it has changed.

Unfortunately, African Americans are disproportionately affected due to racial injustice/tensions and disparities in health care, financial burdens, and the overwhelming school situations with homeschooling while trying to work.

The extensive programs I have developed, the sermons I have written and delivered, the presentations, workshops, conferences, seminars, and other written communications have required deep study, inquiries, investigations, and exploration. I realize the practical use of these skills have strengthened the work that I have been doing for more than 32 years. The research and studies that have been done have been as rewarding as the finished products. Developing case presentations during my clinical internships have also helped to strengthen my skills and have given me tremendous insight to the clients that sit across from me. I provide services at the wonderful place I now work while obtaining my required therapy hours for full licensure. I will also continue to do this work under Isaac Ministries, Inc., my non-profit 501(c) 3 company.

More importantly, throughout my internships many clients I have encountered and counseled have been African American women who have had horrendous traumatic experiences from their early childhood to their emerging adult years. These types of scars run deep, and I have seen the effects and damage it can do to lives, as they have shared their hopelessness, pain, and suffering. Even now, I am still counseling women with varying nationalities and ethnicities who have experienced trauma in their early childhood.

As I shared previously, my deepest scar was from domestic violence. My scars and strengths have assisted me in being able to sit with these clients, hold hope for them, and empathize with them, because I have had the experience of trauma and the desire to be made whole, and right. I can understand the perceived spiritual betrayal and dark places trauma can carry you. The limitations I find are in the areas of scholarly research on African American women. Scholarly research I have found is limited into understanding the plight of African American girls and women who have had traumatic experiences, and hearing our voices as ways of being, understanding, and intervening according to our intercultural traditions, and not cookie cutter practices geared to the dominant cultures' theories. I intend to be a strong voice for inter-culturally sound writing and research that can provide ways of being, ways of understanding, and ways of intervening for African American women and how they can heal. I haven't made it to that doctoral program, yet. I am waiting for God to tell me when, because when He tells me, it will be the right time and the finances will be there to cover it (smile).

Client Evaluations

Henri Nouwen (1979), in his book, The Wounded Healer wrote:

> "Through compassion it is possible to recognize that the craving for love that people feel resides also in our own hearts, that the cruelty the world knows all too well is also rooted in our own impulses. Through compassion we also sense our hope for forgiveness in our friends' eyes and our hatred in their bitter mouths. When they kill, we know that we could have done it; when they give life, we know that we can do the same. For a compassionate person nothing human is alien: no joy and no sorrow, no way of living and no way of dying."

I have counseled with clients who have been diagnosed with Grief and Bereavement, Bipolar Disorders, Attention Deficit Hyperactivity Disorder (ADHD), Major Depression Disorder (MDD), Anxiety, Anger Management, Post Traumatic Stress Disorder, Child Abuse, Relationship Distress, and Spirituality issues. I have served at a homeless shelter, Job Corps, a hospice life center, a clinical center at a university to provide counseling, and a community organization servicing victim of crimes. Regardless of the presenting problems, I found that most clients have experienced early childhood trauma.

Clients come to counseling with stories of sexual trauma that occurred in their lives at very early years. Still others come for grief, but find their past traumatic experiences are exacerbating their grief. Sexual or any type of trauma at young ages establishes adverse child effects for years to come. Trauma informed care is necessary for a client who has experienced trauma because a misstep in their care can retraumatize them.

My work with trauma clients is a lot about building trust, allowing them to tell their story, and empowering them to move towards regaining their sense of safety, identity, and reclaiming their voice. As the therapist, my way of being with the client requires unconditional positive regard, empathic listening, consistency, a genuine relationship, and a connection of soul to soul. The most important way of being is with patience, not rushing, and allowing them to move at their own pace (Cheston, 2014). This allows time for the therapist to understand the event (what happened), how they experienced the event and the effect it has made in their living life after the event. The goal is the client also be able to understand not only the dynamics of the traumatic experience and domestic abuse, but also how the experience from the abuse and other vicarious traumas has impacted them. These important details inform the therapist on how to work with the client and help set goals, based on the client's wishes.

As a Christian pastoral counselor, as well as, a multicultural therapist, I have been able to identify which issues are theological (spiritual), which were theoretical (clinical), and which were the existential issues (meaning making, end of

108

life). Finding the categories pointed to which techniques and interventions would be appropriate. These included relaxation exercises, homework, imagery, and gestalt techniques which were used to: re-establish safety and control, build spiritual practices to help shape spiritual formation by utilizing spiritual affirmations, and the empty chair or writing letters to complete any unfinished business that may still exist as a result of not saying goodbye due to deaths. Psycho-education to correct faulty thinking, carefrontation and behavioral exercises to assist in changing maladaptive behaviors, and journaling in association with mindfulness meditation can increase awareness of the experiences and feelings without judgment. Trauma care can be a long journey ahead using motivational interviewing to track the change cycles and if/when they are ready to work towards the needed changes to live a more productive life.

Critique of Counseling to Date

In all my years of doing ministerial and pastoral work (32 years), trauma clients for me are the most baffling and challenging. I struggle, toil, scratch my head, pray, meditate, and constantly invite God to help me to the do the work needed for their healing. I have had to labor before God to bring clarity, insight, and the ability to get beneath and identify defenses and be able to sit with them and not become overwhelmed or frustrated. I believe I have been able to grow in some areas as a result of doing research, study, reading, and revisiting things I have learned in Pastoral Counseling. As an intern, I have missed cues from the client that I have picked-up on while watching video tapes.

Taking an intercultural approach, understanding the client's cultural make-up, but also other cultural influences that have influenced their development. This was previously a barrier to my successfully working with any client that has been influenced by several cultures. However, this is where research is so important. Also, exploring and researching the epigenetic view of how nature and nurture play a part in human development is another area to be studied and strengthened.

Tamar, who we talked about previously, and her experience of a traumatic rape by her brother was not a case, as told in the bible, that ended well. Reclaiming your life after rape by a stranger, but, by a relative is even more devastating.

Tamar had no guidance, no therapy, or support to help her recover. She received no restitution, but was told to be silent, "hold your peace, don't take it to heart". In other words, don't say anything, don't let it bother you. Victims are often told, "don't tell!" One of the recurring stories or childhood sexual abuse or molestations is that they never told anyone after it happened. Sometimes it is years later before they tell or even remember it happened because it had been repressed, blacked-out of their memory.

Although they carry the memory of the experience, cognitive reasoning in their minds believe they are now worthless, of no value, damaged goods, and useless - like dirty rags - and thrown away. Tamar begged her brother to not shame her but preserve her dignity and respect. Her innocence was stolen like so many of our young girls and boys. Low self-esteem, drinking, drugs, suicide and attempted suicides, sexual promiscuousness, depression and anxiety, are all the effects that can manifest as symptoms of sexual assaults and abuse. Victims also experience powerlessness and a torn spirit that will not heal. Tamar remained desolate in her brother Absalom's house (2 Samuel 13:20).

Rape is not to be taken lightly, not something to simply shrug off. It is violence and a violation that must be reported so victims can experience closure, recovery, self-respect, and justice. The emotional damage is severe. King David, Tamar's father was angry, but he took no action to right the wrong. He didn't even do what the law required, which was force his son to marry Tamar. There was no punishment or rebuke. Perhaps, David's reflection on his own sin with Bathsheba, caused him to feel his own moral authority was not such that he could condemn another (Richards, 1999 pg. 133). Hope of recovery was thwarted by all the men in her life. Remember, women had no rights during this time. Women are still fighting subjugation and equality for their rightful and God given place in this world.

Tamar's story is a reminder that bad things happen to good people. Sometimes those we look to for help and justice will fail us. Only God's grace, mercy, healing, and restorative justice can restore our sense of self-worth and provide fresh and new beginnings. This story also reminds us of the importance of breaking the silence of any and all violence, abuse and assaults. Lastly, we can expose ourselves to vulnerable situations. Although innocent, we can find ourselves alone with people, even a family member, and become a victim. Guard yourself and do not be put in vulnerable situations even with trusted friends and family (Richards, 1999 pg. 134).

There is hope for victims of trauma today. Thank God I live during this time that help is available to hold hope for clients while you walk with them to healing and wholeness. Patience is key if you work with or have a loved one who has experienced trauma. Perhaps who were or are a victim of sexual assault, sexual abuse, molestation, or other forms of trauma. Trauma shapes the survivor's basic beliefs about identity, world view, spirituality, and safety. It is important to establish trust, respect, dignity, and safety with the survivor. The loss of control, the feeling of powerlessness, confidence in self, and all they had ever known, may now be challenged. Their worldview is the world is not a safe place and people are no longer to be trusted. Spiritual beliefs and values are also shaken and are no longer trusted and even God is questionable. Love them until they heal and move beyond the pain. With God, all things are possible. I am a witness.

Conclusion

Scars are the roadmap to the soul, and the soul is where love abides. I am reminded of giving birth to my three children through natural childbirth. The labor and pain of bringing forth new life was an awesome experience and a great privilege that many women desire to have but cannot experience. Like giving birth, a woman endures the pain and exercises patience (as much as she can) in hopeful expectation that the nine months she has carried this new life within her will yield unspeakable joy. The joy that comes after the pain allows her to forget the pain and have more children. The pain that only endures for a while, I liken to the scars I carry. They remind me of the light affliction that was but for a moment, has yielded a harvest of a successful career of pursuing my passion for helping the marginalized, oppressed, and abused. Pain and suffering are never joyous as you are going through such chaos and turmoil. When you sit across from a client in their first session, they narrate their stories of tremendous trauma, pain, and suffering. Conversely, in their termination session, they speak of the healing they have received. They embrace and embody the language of having tools to help them heal, and my scars celebrate the deliverance and freedom they have longed to experience. And it is all worth it. They are who they are supposed to be. And now, I am who I am supposed to be. We have shared the love and connectedness of a therapeutic relationship that has been a roadmap that has led them to their liberation. "There was pain, too, certainly, but love does not think that very significant" (Hurnard, 2012, p. 9).

References

Andrews, D. P. (2002). Practical theology for black churches. Louisville, KY: Westminster John Knox Press.

Ball, M.L. (2007). I'm mad ~~at~~ ^{as} hell, a journey to sanctified, satisfied, and single, Understanding the dynamics of spiritual warfare and domestic violence. 2nd Ed. Columbia, MD:ML Ministries Publishing.

Ball, M.L. (2011). Foundations of theory and practice for helping relationships paper. Unpublished manuscript, Pastoral Counseling Department, Loyola University Maryland, Columbia, MD.

Ball, M.L. (2012). Integrative paper for human development. Unpublished Manuscript, Pastoral Counseling Department, Loyola University Maryland, Columbia, MD.

Ball, M.L. (2014). Case presentation #2 -- Clinical supervision I. Unpublished Manuscript, Pastoral Counseling Department, Loyola University Maryland. Columbia, MD.

Ball, M.L. (2014). Case presentation # 3 – Clinical supervision II. Unpublished Manuscript, Pastoral Counseling Department, Loyola University Maryland. Columbia, MD.

Ball, M. L. (2014). Pastoral integration seminar final paper. Pastoral integration seminar. Unpublished manuscript,

Pastoral Counseling Department, Loyola University Maryland. Columbia, MD.

Ball, M.L. (2014). Psychological testing and assessments final paper. Sections 2-4, pp. 4-11. Unpublished manuscript, Pastoral Counseling Department, Loyola University Maryland, Columbia, MD.

Ball, M.L. (2014). Reflection of the Sacred. Pastoral Integration Seminar. Unpublished manuscript, Pastoral Counseling Department, Loyola University Maryland. Columbia, MD.

Ball, M.L. (2015). Case presentation #6 – Clinical supervision IV. Unpublished manuscript, Pastoral Counseling Department, University Maryland, Columbia, MD.

Cheston, S. (2014). Notes for lecture on trauma. Treatment of psychopathology. Pastoral Counseling Department, Loyola University Maryland, Columbia, MD.

Collins, P.H. (2000). Black feminist thought (2nd ed.). New York: Routledge.

Cooper, D.B. (2013). Hannah Hurnard hinds' feet on high places devotional. The original and complete allegory with devotional. Shippensburg, PA: Destiny Image Publishers, Inc.

Corey, G. (2009). Student manual for theory and practice of counseling and psychotherapy (8th ed.). Belmont: Brooks/Cole Cengage Learning.

Corey, G. (2009). Theory and practice of counseling and psychotherapy (8th ed.). Belmont: Brooks/Cole Cengage Learning.

Driskill, J.D. (2006). Spirituality and the formation of pastoral counselors. *American Journal of Pastoral Counselors.* Vol. 8, No. ¾, pp. 69-85.

E-reading Worksheets, Examples of Metaphors. Retrieved from: http://www.ereadingworksheets.com/figurative-language/figurative-language examples/metaphor-examples/.

Evans, K.M., Kincade, A.F., Marbley, A.F., & Seem, S.R. (2005). Feminism and feminist therapy: Lessons from the past and hopes for the future. *Journal of Counseling and Development, 83.3, p269.*

Fowler, J. W. (1981). Stages of faith, the psychology of human development and the quest for meaning. New York, NY: Harpers Collins Publisher.

Graham, A. M. (2006). Race and ethnicity in the formation of pastoral Counselors. *American Journal of Pastoral Counseling, 8(3),* 87-98. doi: 10.1300/J062v08n03_06.

Hall, C. W. & Webster, R. E. (2007). Risk factors among adult children of alcoholics. *International Journal of Behavioral Consultation and Therapy. 3, 4.*

Hurnard, H. (2012). Hinds' feet in high places. United States: Start Publishing Inc.

Johnson, R. (2013). Spirituality in counseling and psychotherapy. An integrative approach that empowers clients. Hoboken, NJ: John Wiley & Sons, Inc.

Knowles, D., & Bryant, R. M. (2011). African American women counselors, wellness, and spirituality. *Georgia School Counselors Association Journal, 18*(1), 44-47.

Lartey, E. Y. (2003). In living color: an intercultural approach to pastoral care and counseling *(2*nd ed.). London, NY: Jessica Kingsley Publishers.

Mairet, P. (1999). ABC of Adler's psychology. London: Routledge.

Moon, C. and Moon, B. (2007). Workbook and guide for hind's feet on high places. Tyndale House Publishers, Inc.

Nouwen, H. J. M. (1979). The wounded healer, ministry in contemporary society. New York, NY: Doubleday.

Pargament, K. I. (2007). Spiritually integrated psychopathology understanding and addressing the sacred. New York, NY: The Guilford Press.

Piedmont R.L., Toscano M.E. (2016) Assessment of Spirituality and Religious Sentiments (ASPIRES) Scale. In: Zeigler-Hill V., Shackelford T. (eds) Encyclopedia of Personality and Individual Differences. Springer, Cham.

Piedmont, R. L. (2014). Assessment of spirituality and religious sentiments scoring and interpretive computer report. Psychological testing and assessment. Pastoral Counseling Department, Loyola University Maryland, Columbia, MD.

Piedmont, R. L. (2014) Notes for lecture on Logoplex: A model for making personal meaning. Psychological testing and assessments/. Pastoral Counseling Department, Loyola University Maryland, Columbia, MD.

Rath, T. (2007). StrengthsFinder 2.0. New York, NY: Gallup Press.

Richards, L. and S. (1999). Every woman in the Bible, fully illustrated. Nashville, TN: Thomas Nelson Publishers.

Santrock, J.W. (2011). Life span development *(*13th ed.*)*. New York, NY: McGaw-Hill.

Scar. (2010). In Microsoft online thesaurus.

Sicking, J. S. (2011). Notes for lecture on Adlerian counseling and critical constructivist theories. Theory and practice. Pastoral Counseling Department, Columbia, MD: Loyola University Maryland.

Stassen, G.H., Gushee, D.P. (2003). Kingdom ethics. Downers Grove, IL: InterVarsity Press.

Tisdale, T. C., Doehring, C. E., & Lorraine-Poirier, V. L. (2003). Three voices, one song: a psychologist, spiritual director, and pastoral counselor share perspectives on providing care. *Journal of Psychology and Theology, Vol. 31, No. 1*, 52-68.

Unalienable Rights Defined. Retrieved from:
http://www.unalienable.com/unalien.htm.

Welling, H. (2005). Intuition and counseling. *Journal of Psychotherapy Integration. Vol. 15, No. 1*, pp 19-47. Educational Publishing Foundation. 1053-0479/05/$12.00 DOI: 10.1037/1053-0479.15.1.19.

Wiggins, M.I. (2009). Therapist self-awareness of spirituality. 53-74. American Psychological Associations. Washington, DC: US.

Willis, A. (1996). The disciple's victory masterlife. Nashville, TN: LifeWay Press.

Wimberly, E.P. (1999). Moving from shame to self-worth: Preaching and pastoral care. Tennessee: Abingdon Press.